Trient Press®

Copyright © 2023 by Trient Press

Trient Press
3375 S Rainbow Blvd
#81710, SMB 13135
Las Vegas,NV 89180

Ordering Information:
Quantity sales. Special discounts are available on quantity purchases by corporations, associations, and others. For details, contact the publisher at the address above.
Orders by U.S. trade bookstores and wholesalers. Please contact Trient Press: Tel: (775) 996-3844; or visit www.trientpress.com.

Printed in the United States of America

Publisher's Cataloging-in-Publication data
Trient Press
A title of a book : Trientrepreneur

BY: TIERELL GOODMAN

O
F
F

THE

PATH

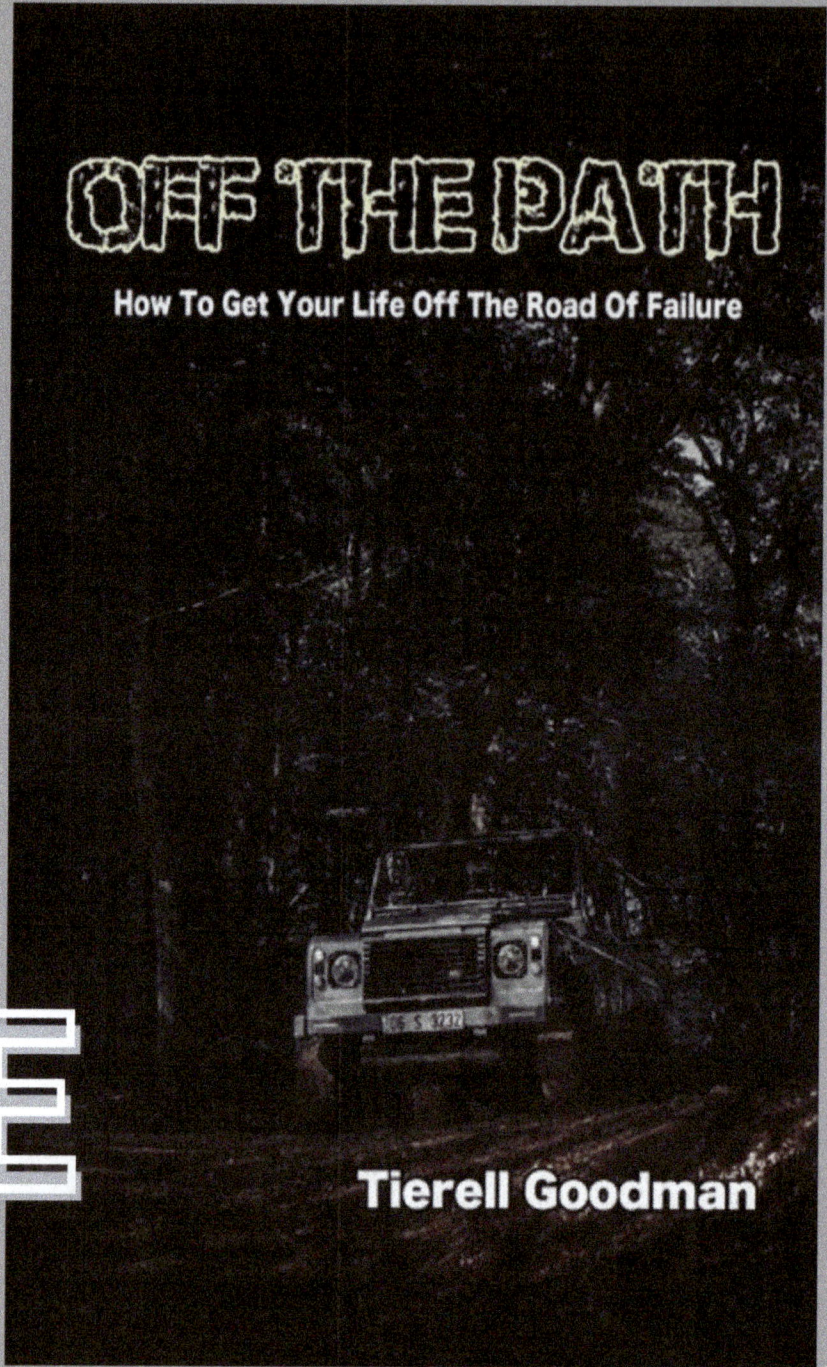

OFF THE PATH
How To Get Your Life Off The Road Of Failure

Tierell Goodman

Trient Press®

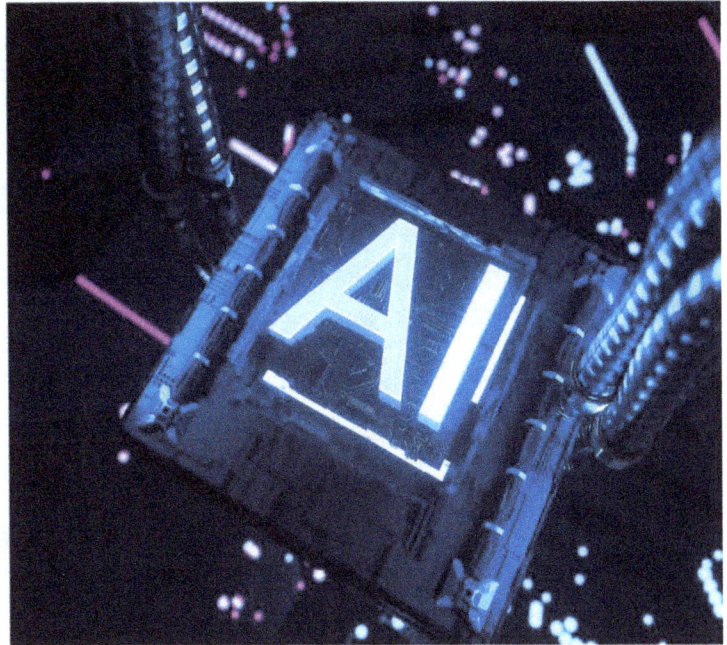

TRIENTREPRENEUR

ISSUE 14

Editor-in-Chief
Head Staff-Writer
Melisa Ruscsak

Managing Editor
Graphic Design Editor
Kristina Wenzl-Figueroa

Trient Press®

SEPTEMBER/ OCTOBER AUTHOR TIPS

Author's Alchemy: Merging AI with Creativity for Enhanced Success

- Embrace AI Writing Tools: Utilize AI-driven writing and editing tools to enhance creativity and efficiency in content creation.
- Leverage Data Analytics: Employ AI algorithms for analyzing reader behavior and preferences, enabling personalized marketing and content strategies.

- Automate Administrative Tasks: Use AI-powered automation for routine tasks like scheduling, freeing up time for creative endeavors.

- Explore AI in Publishing: Investigate AI-driven platforms that can match your manuscripts with appropriate publishers or help in self-publishing.

- Enhance User Engagement: Utilize chatbots and AI-driven interfaces to foster interactive and personalized experiences for your readers.

- Utilize Predictive Analytics: Apply AI in forecasting book sales and trends, assisting in inventory management and strategic planning.

- Improve Accessibility: Incorporate AI-powered voice and translation services to make your content accessible to a broader audience.

- Secure Intellectual Property: Employ AI in plagiarism checks and copyright management to protect your creative works.

- Enhance Cover Design: Utilize AI-driven design tools for creating eye-catching and genre-appropriate book covers.

- Integrate with Social Media Marketing: Leverage AI algorithms to analyze and optimize social media advertising, targeting the right audience for your books.

A Bridge of Magic Novel

THE
STRUGGLE
FOR
INNOCENCE

ROBERT E. BALSLEY, JR.

ILLUSTRATED BY JIM CHARLES AND SHELLEY CHARLES

Trient Press®

LIGHTS, CAMERA, AI:

The New Frontier in Filmmaking

NEWS PROVIDED BY: Trient Press

Historical Overview of AI in Cinema

Remember those classic movies with chunky, clunky robots or super-smart computers? They seemed so far out, right? Like, totally make-believe. Well, guess what? Some of that make-believe stuff isn't just in the land of pretend anymore.

Let me take you back a bit. Imagine sitting in a dim-lit cinema, munching on popcorn, and watching a sci-fi movie. There's a scene where a robot is talking or a computer is thinking by itself. You'd think, "Wow, that's cool, but we're ages away from that." That was the magic of movies: making the impossible look real.

Fast-forward to now. Surprise! Those magical movie moments aren't just in films. They're here with us. Today, those big ideas are not just on the big screen. They're behind the scenes, too. AI isn't just a character in movies; it's helping make them. Cameras? They've got AI. The way films are edited? Yep, AI's there. And the stories? Some are even being thought up by AI!

It's like we've jumped into one of those futuristic movies. Only, this isn't make-believe. It's our world now. The dreamers who made those old films might be amazed to see what's happening. I know I am. How about you?

It's like we've jumped into one of those futuristic movies. Only, this isn't make-believe. It's our world now. The dreamers who made those old films might be amazed to see what's happening. I know I am. How about you? And speaking of stories, think about the power they have to draw us in. Imagine that power combined with the smarts of AI. Exciting, right? But it's not just about the thrill. With AI stepping into the world of tales and drama, we're looking at a mix of endless opportunities and a handful of challenges. Ready to explore this blend of narrative and tech?.

AI Through The Lens Of Filmmaking

AI and Creative Storytelling: Opportunities and Challenges

If stories are the heartbeat of our culture. AI might just be the fresh rhythm giving it a new life.

The Magic of Collaboration

You know how a brilliant film can transport you to a different world or how a gripping book can keep you up all night? Now, imagine adding a sprinkle of AI magic to that experience. We're not talking about robots writing novels or directing movies. It's about the collaboration between human creativity and machine intelligence, and it's transforming how we create and consume stories.

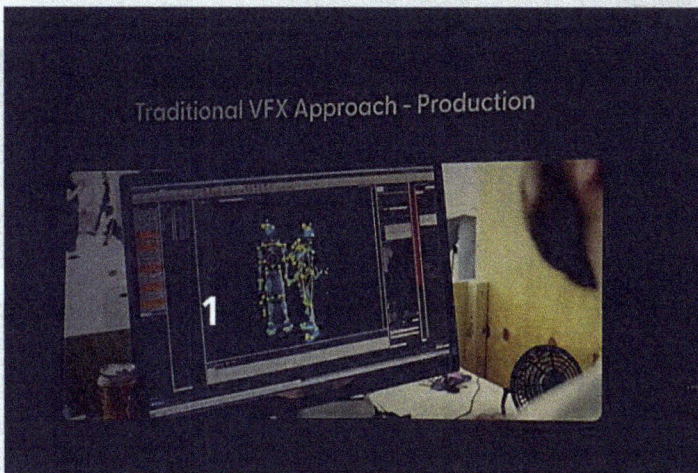

Traditional VFX Approach - Production

The Opportunities:

- *Customization* - AI can analyze individual preferences, tailoring content to resonate with each person. Ever wanted a story that feels like it was written just for you? That might soon be a reality.

- *Innovative Narratives* - AI can suggest plot twists or character developments that a human might not think of. Imagine a storyline that evolves based on real-world events or audience reactions.

- *Efficiency in Production* - From script revisions to post-production edits, AI tools can speed up the filmmaking process, making the creation more efficient without compromising on quality.

The Challenges

- *Losing the Human Touch* - While AI can suggest, it might lack the emotional depth and nuance that human storytellers bring. A machine might not understand the subtle emotions of heartbreak or the exhilaration of adventure in the same way we do.

- *Over-reliance* - Relying too much on AI might stifle originality. We wouldn't want every story to feel like it was churned out of the same mold, would we?

- *Ethical Dilemmas* - Who gets the credit for a story co-written by AI and a human? And how do we handle biases that AI might introduce into narratives?

The Road Ahead

The blend of AI and storytelling is like a new genre in the making. It's thrilling, a bit mysterious, and packed with potential. While we embrace the benefits, it's essential to tread thoughtfully, ensuring stories remain as diverse, emotional, and human as they've always been. After all, in the interplay between tech and tales, the heart of storytelling should always shine brightest.

Ethics and Representation in AI-Driven Filmmaking

When Computers Get the Director's Chair...

Remember the last time you sat down to watch a movie and thought, "Hey, this feels familiar?" Well, with computers helping make movies now, that could happen more often. But why?

Learning from the Past

Computers, or AI, learn from old movies to make new ones. So, if they're watching the same famous actors and hearing the same stories, guess what they'll want to create? Yep, more of the same.

But, Isn't Fair Always Square?

Here's the thing. If AI keeps picking the same actors or the same type of stories, it's kinda like always eating vanilla ice cream. We'd miss out on all the other amazing flavors! That's why many folks worry AI might leave out new voices, fresh tales, or folks who don't always make the headlines.

Teaching Computers Heart and Soul

However, not all hope is lost. Filmmakers are trying to teach AI about fairness. It's like teaching a little kid about sharing toys or playing nice. They're trying to help AI understand that movies aren't just about big stars. They're about real feelings, dreams, and sometimes, even the little guy in the corner who has an epic tale to share.

And What About Us?

While computers learn, we can help too. By supporting different kinds of stories and filmmakers, we send a message about what we want to watch. And guess what? AI is listening.

In a Nutshell

AI in movies? It's cool but needs some guidance. Kinda like a teenager learning to drive. With a bit of care, patience, and teaching, we can enjoy the ride and still make sure everyone gets a turn at the wheel.

Harnessing the Power of Social Media:

Social media platforms have become indispensable tools for authors to connect directly with readers, build relationships, and generate buzz around their work. From sharing book updates to behind-the-scenes glimpses into the writing process, authors can leverage platforms like Instagram, Twitter, and Facebook to engage with their audience, host giveaways, and collaborate with influencers or fellow authors to expand their reach.

Rolling Credits on Our AI Adventure

The Final Scene...

You ever sit through the ending credits of a movie? It's that long list of names and jobs. Well, think of AI as a new name on that list. And it's getting a starring role.

New Kid on the Block: AI Enters the Scene

The Schoolyard of Cinema
Picture a bustling school playground. There's the sound of laughter, the

AI is like the new kid at school that everyone is curious about but afraid to befriend at first.

energy of games, and little groups forming everywhere. This playground is like the world of movies. Each group, each kid, has a role. There are the actors – always in the limelight, practicing their lines and expressions. The directors – they've got the vision, guiding the games and setting the rules. And then, the writers – daydreaming, scribbling ideas in their notebooks, and weaving stories.

Enter AI: The Newcomer
Then one day, the school bell rings, and in walks AI, the new kid with shiny techy shoes and a brain full of codes. This kid is different, buzzing with ideas and bringing a backpack full of tools that can change how games are played. Everyone's curious. Some kids run over, eager to see what AI can do. Can it help them act better? Direct cooler scenes? Write more exciting tales?

Mixed Feelings in the Playground
But not all are thrilled. There's a group, a tad wary, watching from a distance. They whisper, "What if this new kid changes our games? What if it doesn't understand the heart and soul of our stories?" They've heard rumors - about AI preferring certain stories over others or not really "getting" emotions.

Fitting In and Finding Balance
Like any new kid, AI wants to fit in. It's here to help, to enhance, not to replace. With a little guidance, it can understand what the playground wants. But, it needs the other kids to teach it, to show it the ropes. It's a team effort.

Game Changer?
Will AI change the way movies are made? Maybe. Will it bring a fresh perspective? Definitely. But one thing's for sure: the playground's gotten a lot more interesting.

The Good, The Bad, and The Techie:
AI's Cinematic Journey

Opening Scene: The Good

Enter AI, the tech whiz of the cinematic world. With its speedy calculations and vast knowledge, movies are now being made quicker and, in some ways, even smarter. It can analyze audience reactions in a heartbeat, suggesting tweaks and changes to make a film more engaging. It's like having a super-smart friend who's always up for a movie marathon and can guess what the audience will love next.

Act Two: The Bad

But like any intriguing plot twist, AI isn't flawless. Remember your first time on a bike? The wobbles, the uncertainty, the falls. AI's sort of in that clumsy stage. Sometimes, it gets stuck in a loop, picking the same popular stories it thinks everyone wants. It can be like that friend who keeps recommending the same type of movie over and over, not realizing there's a whole world of genres out there.

The Climax: The Techie's Potential

However, just as you didn't give up on biking after a few tumbles, AI's story isn't over after a few hiccups. With the right guidance – think of it as training wheels – AI can explore fresh narratives. It can dive deep into its vast database, unearthing hidden gems and forgotten tales, or even suggesting entirely new storylines.

The Grand Finale

So, while our techie newcomer has its strengths and flaws, it holds promise. A promise of a cinema landscape that's dynamic, diverse, and ever-evolving. With filmmakers and AI working hand in hand, who knows the limit to the stories we'll see?

The Audience's Role

That's us! We're like the movie fans with popcorn in hand, waiting to see what happens next. We can cheer for the great stuff and give a thumbs-down to things we don't like. By choosing the kind of movies we watch and support, we're kind of directing AI too.

And... Cut!

So, as the lights dim and the curtains fall, one thing's clear: the movie world's got a new player. And it's up to us, the fans, to make sure it brings out the best in cinema. Just like in movies, every character has a role to play, and this story? Well, it's just getting started.

DATA SCIENCE

Digital Darwinism: How Natural Selection Shapes Artificial Intelligence

Ever watched kids play the classic game, King of the Hill? It's a scramble to the top, where only the toughest stay standing. Nature has a game just like that, it's called "natural selection." The idea? The best-adapted animals and plants thrive while others take a back seat. But here's a twist for you, the digital world plays this game too.

Welcome to the age of Digital Darwinism.

From Jungle to Java: Navigating the Dense Digital Forest

Venture into the realm of our digital universe, and it parallels the intricacies of a thriving jungle. Here, amidst the thickets of data and towering algorithms, lies Artificial Intelligence (AI), a transformative force growing and evolving each passing moment.

At its heart, the world of AI is as diverse as the inhabitants of a jungle. Just as in nature, where not every creature is equipped for every challenge, AI models vary significantly in their capabilities. Neural networks, for instance, are like the leopards of our digital jungle—swift, adaptive, and capable of deep learning. They can sift through vast amounts of data, recognize patterns, and make predictions.

Then there are decision trees, akin to the wise old owls perched high. They make calculated decisions, branching out in numerous directions based on the data they're given. Machine learning algorithms, on the other hand, are like the ants—constantly at work, adjusting, and refining their routes and strategies based on past experiences.

However, as robust and impressive as these AI models are, they are not infallible. Some might excel in crunching numbers and predicting stock market trends but might struggle with natural language processing or visual recognition. That's akin to the lion—undeniably majestic and powerful in its territory but requiring to adapt when the landscape changes.

Languages like Java, Python, or R are the lifeblood of this digital jungle, enabling these AI models to function, learn, and grow. They provide the nourishment, much like the rivers and sunlight in a natural jungle, ensuring that our digital fauna thrives.

But as with all ecosystems, balance is key. In our vast digital forest, it is up to us—developers, ethicists, and users—to ensure this equilibrium. We need to nurture the AI, train it, prune its excesses, and guide its growth, ensuring it doesn't become the unchecked king of the jungle but remains a vital and harmonious part of the ecosystem.

The Seesaw of Success: The Delicate Dance of Digital Evolution

In the vast playground of the digital domain, success is ever-fleeting, operating on a delicate balance reminiscent of a seesaw. On one end, we might find a software tool, perhaps

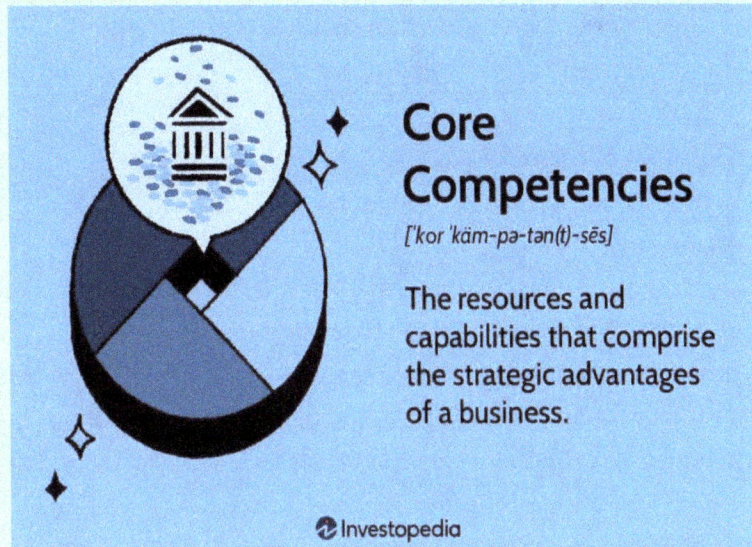

Core Competencies
[ˈkor ˈkäm-pə-tən(t)-sēs]

The resources and capabilities that comprise the strategic advantages of a business.

Investopedia

written in Python or Java, dominating the market due to its cutting-edge features. Its algorithms might be adept at pattern recognition, allowing for predictive analytics that businesses find invaluable. It's riding high, casting a long shadow on the ground.

Yet, in this rapidly evolving world, being on top today does not guarantee a position there tomorrow. With the introduction of advanced neural networks and deep learning techniques, another software could emerge, one that is far more efficient, or possibly built on a newer framework like TensorFlow or PyTorch. This software might not only recognize patterns but also intuitively adapt to user behaviors, process massive datasets in real-time, or implement state-of-the-art natural language processing capabilities. As it gains traction, our seesaw begins to shift.

The dynamism of the AI landscape ensures continuous evolution. For AI systems, this adaptation is akin to the way animals adjust to changing climates or landscapes. Genetic algorithms, for instance, mirror the process of natural selection. They iterate upon themselves, "breeding" optimal solutions over time by merging and mutating potential answers to a problem.

An AI solution that once reigned supreme might find itself outperformed by another that has gone through numerous cycles of such self-optimization

.But what of the software and AI models that resist adaptation, or simply can't keep pace? They gradually recede into the background. These once-revered tools start to feel like legacy systems, analogous to those cherished but long-forgotten toys relegated to the dusty corners of an attic. They serve as a testament to a time gone by, reminding us of where we've been and just how fast the digital world propels forward.

As developers, businesses, and users, understanding this ever-shifting balance is crucial. Today's dominant solution might be tomorrow's relic. Investing time and resources in constant learning, adaptation, and forward-thinking can ensure a steadier position on this relentless digital seesaw.

We're the Park Rangers: Navigating the Digital Ecosystem

Amid the sprawling expanse of the digital jungle, brimming with the complexity of algorithms, neural networks, and endless lines of code, there's an empowering realization: we're not mere bystanders. Instead, we play the role of vigilant park rangers, maintaining order and balance within this intricate ecosystem.

Like seasoned rangers who understand the intricacies of the forests they oversee, we possess the unique expertise to harness and navigate the technological advances before us. With tools like machine learning libraries TensorFlow and Scikit-learn, or languages such as Python and R, we can train our AI systems.

We determine the datasets they process, the parameters they operate within, and ultimately, the outcomes they yield.

Consider the role of reinforcement learning in AI – a technique where machines are taught to make decisions by rewarding them for correct choices and penalizing for incorrect ones. It's akin to training a wild animal in our vast digital park, guiding its behavior until it aligns with our desired objectives.

But this responsibility extends beyond mere technical calibration. We are the bearers of ethical and moral compasses, holding the power to infuse these values into our artificial entities. When we come across biases in machine learning models, for example, we can fine-tune these systems, ensuring they make decisions devoid of prejudices. We have frameworks like Fairness Indicators and tools like IBM's AI Fairness 360 to assist in this task, checking and recalibrating our models to uphold the principles of equity and justice.

Ultimately, the balance of the digital seesaw is a collective responsibility. With every algorithm we design, every neural network we deploy, and every line of code we write, we are actively determining the orientation of this balance. By being vigilant, ethical, and technically adept, we can ensure that the digital terrain remains robust, inclusive, and forward-facing, truly representative of the ideals we cherish.

The Future Playground: Balancing Innovation with Stewardship

Our current era, fueled by rapid technological advancements, often feels like we're aboard a bullet-train, with Artificial Intelligence (AI) acting as the locomotive propelling us forward. Yet, as we find ourselves engrossed in the marvels of AI-driven innovations – from facial recognition systems in smartphones to predictive analytics in healthcare – it's crucial that we remain active stewards of this burgeoning landscape.

agreements, with AI algorithms aiding in monitoring and verification processes. This seamless amalgamation exemplifies the symbiotic relationship between varied technological domains.

However, Digital Darwinism isn't solely an arena for fierce competition, where the most advanced tech outpaces its peers. It's a collaborative space. A playground, if you will, where human

AI's neural networks are modeled after the human brain.

Consider the vast neural networks that underpin many of AI's functionalities. These are complex systems modeled after the human brain, consisting of layers upon layers of interconnected nodes. Tools such as TensorFlow and Keras help developers train these networks, refining their capabilities. But with this immense power comes the imperative to employ it judiciously. After all, these models are only as good as the data fed into them, and a biased dataset could lead to skewed outcomes. Herein lies our role as the 'gardeners' – diligently pruning any anomalies, ensuring our tech not only grows but flourishes responsibly.

Furthermore, as blockchain technologies gain traction, offering decentralized and transparent systems, AI can be integrated to bolster security and efficiency. Smart contracts on platforms like Ethereum can automatically execute contractual

ingenuity partners with machine capabilities. As quantum computing, set to exponentially boost computational power, gradually becomes a reality, AI will encounter new avenues to explore, learn, and grow. But it will always require human guidance to ensure its evolution is aligned with societal values and needs.

The next time you find yourself engrossed in your favorite AI-powered app, reflect on its intricate journey – the code, the algorithms, the ethical considerations – that catapulted it to your device's screen. For in this vast playground of the future, every player, whether human or digital, has a role. And collectively, we shape the narrative of this exhilarating game.

M.L. Ruscsak

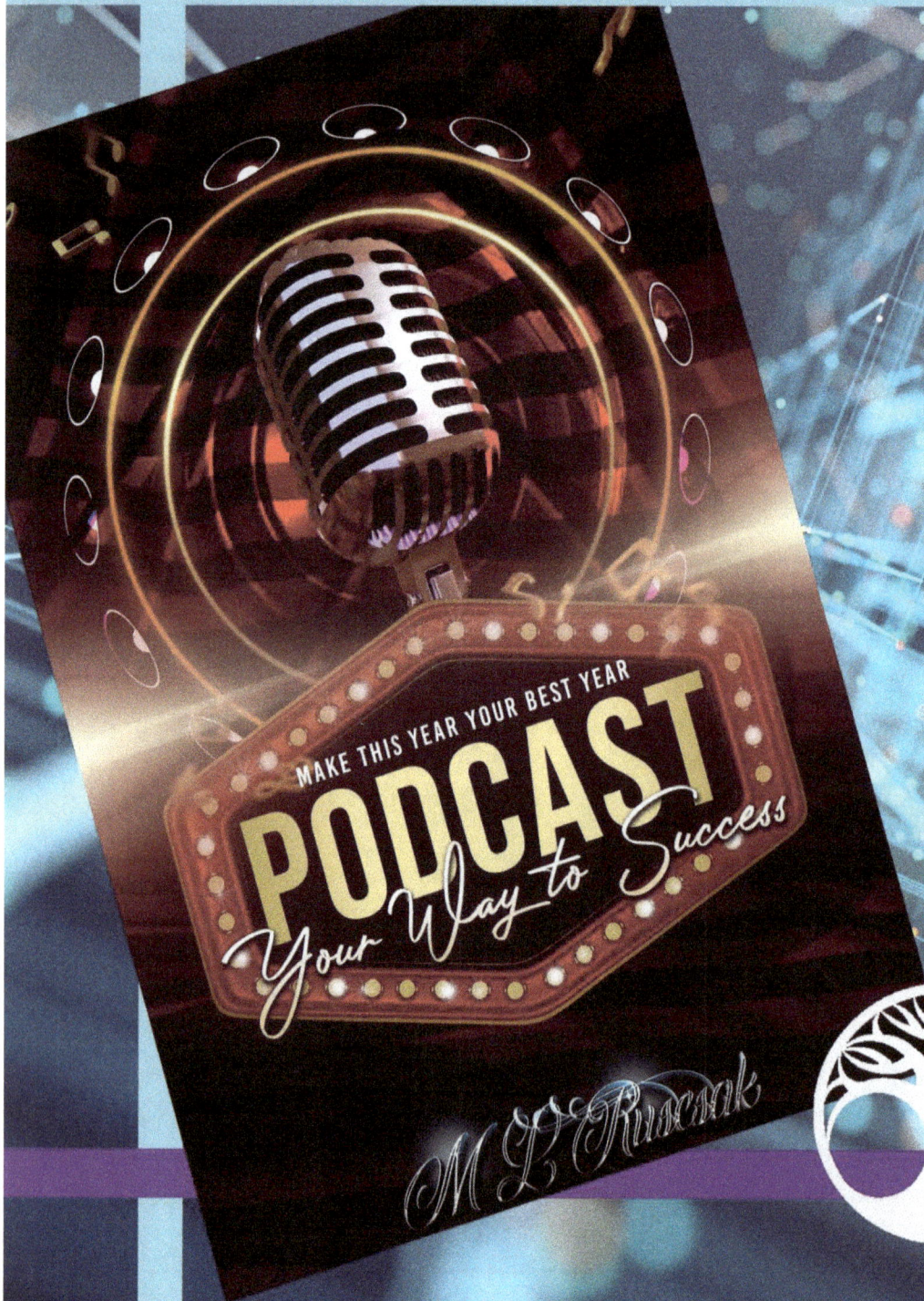

MAKE THIS YEAR YOUR BEST YEAR
PODCAST
Your Way to Success

M.L. Ruscsak

Trient Press

Futures Crafted in Code:
The Venture Capital Lens on AI Innovations

Ever gazed at your phone and thought, "How the heck does this thing know what I'm thinking?" Well, it's a little thing called AI. And behind it? A world of folks believing in dreams built on ones and zeroes.

Magic. But Make it Code: Behind the Algorithmic Curtain

Let's dive deeper into this enchantment. Remember the magic spells in fairy tales? The sorcerer murmurs some words, and voilà, a frog becomes a prince. Well, in the tech realm, those magic spells are coded in languages like Python, Java, or R.

When you scribble a note, it's personal. It has your thoughts, emotions, maybe even a doodle of that dreamy ice cream cone you're craving. Now, what if you could whisper to the universe and make that doodle come alive? AI developers, in a way, are making this happen – only, with a more technological spin.

Imagine they're using a special kind of ink, made up of algorithms. These algorithms are sets of instructions, like a recipe. So, when an AI developer "scribbles a note" (writes code), they're following and inventing recipes.

And these aren't just any recipes – they're the kind that can take a simple idea and transform it into a useful tool, like voice assistants that play your favorite song when asked or apps that can predict the weather down to the minute.

But where's the paper for this magical ink? It's in the digital cloud and our devices. This "paper" captures the ink, understands it, and brings it to life. That's your device's processors and memory at work.

So, the next time your phone app suggests the quickest route home or your smart fridge tells you to buy milk, remember: it started as a scribble, a digital recipe. And thanks to our modern-day wizards (AI developers), they're turning tech doodles into tangible, helpful wonders.

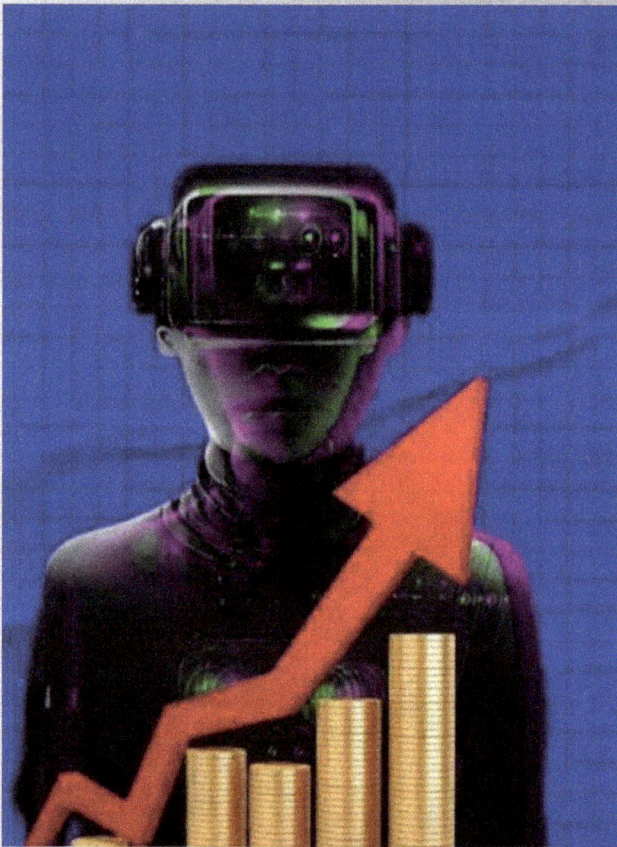

Enter the Money Folks: The Fuel Behind Technological Marvels

Behind every transformative tech marvel, there's not just a line of code but also a story of belief, trust, and investment. Crafting these innovative codes requires more than just a savvy developer with a laptop. There's infrastructure, research, marketing, and so much more involved.

Enter venture capitalists, the unseen powerhouses of the tech industry.

Picture this: a bright young developer has a groundbreaking idea. They can visualize it, can almost touch it, but to bring this vision to life requires more than just enthusiasm. This is where venture capitalists (VCs) come into play. Think of them as the fairy godparents or the patrons of the Renaissance, only for the tech world.

They don't just bring in money. They bring a network, industry insights, and a certain credibility. Venture capitalists evaluate the potential of startups, diving deep into the tech specifics. Is this new AI algorithm truly revolutionary? Does this software solution fill a gap in the market? They examine business models, scrutinize scalability, and even evaluate the team's strength.

Once they spot that golden potential, they invest. But their involvement doesn't end with writing a check. They mentor, guide, and sometimes even help in steering the company's direction. With their financial backing, startups can afford top-tier tech infrastructures, cloud solutions for vast data processing, or even quantum computing capabilities, which are vital in AI calculations.

So, the next time you marvel at an AI innovation, remember it's not just tech magic. It's also the result of a gamble, a belief by someone who saw potential and was willing to stake money on its success. Venture capitalists are the force that can propel an idea from a notebook scribble to a global sensation.

Why Venture Capitalists Heart AI:
The Tech Revolution with Limitless Potential

- Venture Capitalists, often called VCs, are always on the hunt for the next big thing. The recent darling of their eyes? Artificial Intelligence (AI). But what makes AI so special in their eyes? Let's dive deep.

At its core, AI isn't just a new gadget or a simple software upgrade. Instead, think of it as a revolutionary force, akin to the invention of electricity or the internet. It's the new kid on the block who isn't just content with being novel; it wants to revamp the whole neighborhood.

- *A Multifaceted Dynamo:* Like a prodigy who excels in arts, sports, and academics all at once, AI has multiple applications. It can predict stock market trends, make medical diagnoses, enhance video game experiences, and even automate mundane tasks in industries. It's not just about making machines think; it's about making them think in a multitude of ways.

- *The Data Goldmine:* In the age of information, data is the new gold. AI can sift through massive data sets, picking out patterns and insights that might take humans years to discern. This data-crunching capability is invaluable for industries ranging from finance to marketing.

- *Always Evolving:* Unlike static technologies, AI keeps learning and evolving. It's self-improving, using its mistakes and successes to be better, faster, and more efficient. This continuous growth trajectory is a magnet for VCs.

- *The Economic Ripple Effect:* AI's influence is vast. It's not just about one product or service. It can boost productivity, create new markets, and even spawn entirely new sectors. For a venture capitalist, this means multiple avenues of investment and returns.

- *Changing Consumer Behavior:* Remember when online shopping was a novelty? AI is transforming consumer behaviors in similar profound ways. From voice assistants helping with shopping lists to chatbots providing instant customer service – AI is reshaping the consumer landscape.

So, when venture capitalists look at AI, they don't just see a tech trend. They see a seismic shift, a revolution waiting to happen. It's akin to having an insider friend who not only knows the coolest spots in town but is also on the cusp of creating entirely new cities of the future.

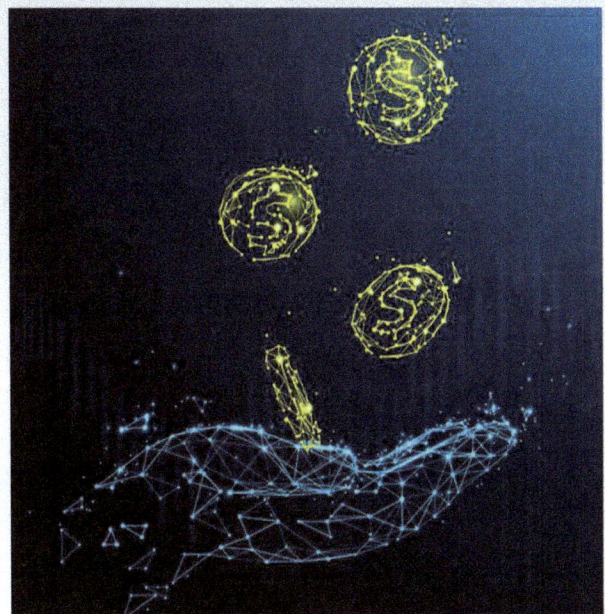

The Crystal Ball Question: Decoding the AI Horizon

Peering into the future of technology, especially AI, is akin to looking into a digital crystal ball. It's misty, unpredictable, yet holds an allure that's irresistible. Let's put on our tech visionary hats and imagine the potential.

- *Neural Interfaces and Thought-Driven Devices:* Brain-computer interfaces (BCIs) might sound like science fiction, but they're closer to reality than we think. Elon Musk's Neuralink is just one example of companies delving into connecting our brains directly to computers. In a decade or so, typing a text or swiping on your phone might be as archaic as using a rotary phone. Fancy ordering a pizza? Just think about it, and your AI-driven device may place the order for you.

- *AI Companions:* With advancements in conversational AI and robotics, we might soon have AI companions that are more than just voice assistants. Imagine a digital pal that knows your favorite movies, listens to your day's highs and lows, and even cracks a joke to cheer you up. Companies like OpenAI and Boston Dynamics are paving the way, merging high-end robotics with intricate AI algorithms.

- *Predictive Personalization:* AI's predictive capabilities are set to be supercharged in the coming years. The music or movie recommendation of today is just the tip of the iceberg. From predicting your mood swings and providing emotional support to foreseeing potential health issues based on your habits, AI will be several steps ahead, making life smoother and more intuitive.

....And Scene: From Dreams to Digital Realities

Behind the seemingly effortless tech marvels are nights of coding, countless debugging sessions, and the relentless pursuit of innovation. And fueling these dreams? A synergy of visionaries, coding wizards, and the financial muscle of backers who see the potential in every line of code.

So, the next time Siri, Alexa, or any other AI-driven tool hits the right note, making your day just a bit better, take a moment. Reflect on the marvel that it is – a blend of human genius, technological prowess, and the spirit of constantly pushing the envelope.

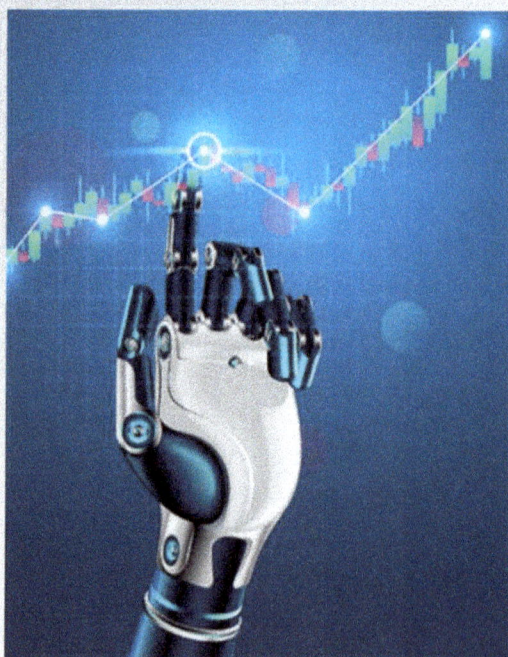

" Assembly of Wanderers

Join us in navigating life's complexities, as we collectively shift from a reactive to a proactive mindset, replacing blame and expectation with gratitude and love, and realizing that within each of us lies the potential for unparalleled achievement, deep fulfillment, and a truly extraordinary quality of life.cumsan lacus vel facilisis.

WANDERCON

17-22 MARCH

FOR MORE INFORMATION VISIT : wandercon.assemblyofwanderers.com

Prepare to be inspired and transformed! Join us with a lineup of luminaries:

⭐ Master Trainer: Antonio T. Smith Jr.

🎤 Celebrity Speaker: Liffort Hobley

💎 Keynote Maestros: Sheena Kerley, Deaunna Marie, Law Loadholt, and Tracey Armstrong.

An unparalleled assembly of brilliance awaits. Ensure your presence in this intellectual symposium—reserve swiftly, as seating is limited.

Awaken your spirit, and enhance the beauty within.

ENTREPRENEUR TIPS AND TRICKS

Digital Handshakes: AI-Enhanced Networking from Dawn to Dusk

- Start with Clear Goals: Before diving into AI networking tools, outline what you want to achieve. Whether it's finding new partners, customers, or investors, a clear goal helps tailor the AI's capabilities to your needs.

- Choose the Right Platform: AI-powered networking isn't one-size-fits-all. Different platforms cater to different needs. LinkedIn might be great for B2B networking, while Clubhouse or Twitter might be more suitable for casual, yet impactful, interactions.

- Personalization is Key: AI can analyze vast amounts of data to tailor interactions. Use this to send personalized messages or offers, making digital handshakes more memorable.

- Stay Updated: AI evolves rapidly. Make it a habit to periodically check for updates or new features in your networking tools. This ensures you're always using the platform's full potential.

- Use Predictive Analysis: Some AI tools can predict which contacts might be most responsive or valuable to you. Leverage this to prioritize your networking efforts.

- Embrace Virtual Events: With AI, virtual events can become highly interactive, replicating the in-person networking experience. Platforms like Hopin or Zoom, integrated with AI, can help attendees match with potential collaborators or clients.

- Maintain Human Touch: While AI can facilitate introductions, building relationships still requires genuine human interaction. Use AI as an introductory tool, not a replacement for meaningful conversations.

- Mind Your Digital Etiquette: Automated doesn't mean impersonal. Avoid spamming or over-automating. It's essential to strike a balance between efficiency and authenticity.

- Protect Data and Privacy: Using AI means dealing with data. Ensure you're transparent about how you handle and protect data, adhering to regulations like GDPR.

- Feedback Loop: Just as you'd seek feedback after an in-person event, use AI analytics to understand what's working and what's not in your digital networking endeavors. Refine your strategies based on these insights.

BEYOND THE HYPE: GROUNDING AI TRANSFORMATIONS IN REAL-WORLD SOLUTIONS

NEWS PROVIDED BY: TRIENT PRESS

"AI's here and it's changing the game!" That's something you've probably heard more times than you can count. But let's go beyond the flashy headlines and neon lights, and talk shop with someone who knows a thing or two about the world of AI – Simon Harris.

Envision this: In a modern workspace, a high-powered computer processes vast amounts of data at lightning speeds, executing algorithms that would boggle the human mind. But there, across the room, a strategist is engrossed in crafting a blueprint, aiming to leverage this computational prowess to elevate the business.

It's clear: the narrative isn't about AI overshadowing humans; it's about a harmonious synergy between them.

Every enterprise, irrespective of its scale, can harness this collaboration. It's not tied to financial might or sprawling headquarters. The foundation rests on four pivotal pillars:

- **High-Quality Data:** This is the fuel for AI. Richer the data, the more robust the AI's performance.

- **Skill-Based** AI: AI systems are diverse. Some excel in niche areas while others have broader capabilities. Identifying the right fit is crucial.
- **Infrastructure:** The backbone of it all. A robust technological framework ensures seamless AI integration and operations.
- Strategy: Here, the brilliance of human innovation comes into play, weaving together the components into a cohesive plan.

To perceive AI merely as a cutting-edge tool would be an oversimplification. It's akin to a sapling that, with the right nourishment – data in this context – blossoms. And the key to unlocking its potential? Comprehending its capabilities and aligning them with the enterprise's goals. The brilliance it radiates? That's catalyzed by the touch of human insight.

A transformation is on the horizon. As AI capabilities advance, generating intricate content and visuals, our professional landscape will undeniably shift. But this doesn't spell obsolescence for us. Instead, our roles metamorphose.

In a future landscape, imagine repetitive tasks being seamlessly managed by AI. Mundanities like data logging or file categorizations become automated. And us? We're at the forefront, pioneering, ideating, and sculpting visionary strategies.

It's evident that the journey ahead isn't about AI monopolizing the stage. It's about a collaborative performance. So, when whispers arise about AI dominance, recall: it's a collaborative performance, and together, we're orchestrating a symphony. ♪♫

GUARDIANS OF SYNTAX:
CalypsoAi's Role
IN SAFEGUARDING LINGUISTICS FOR ENTERPRISES

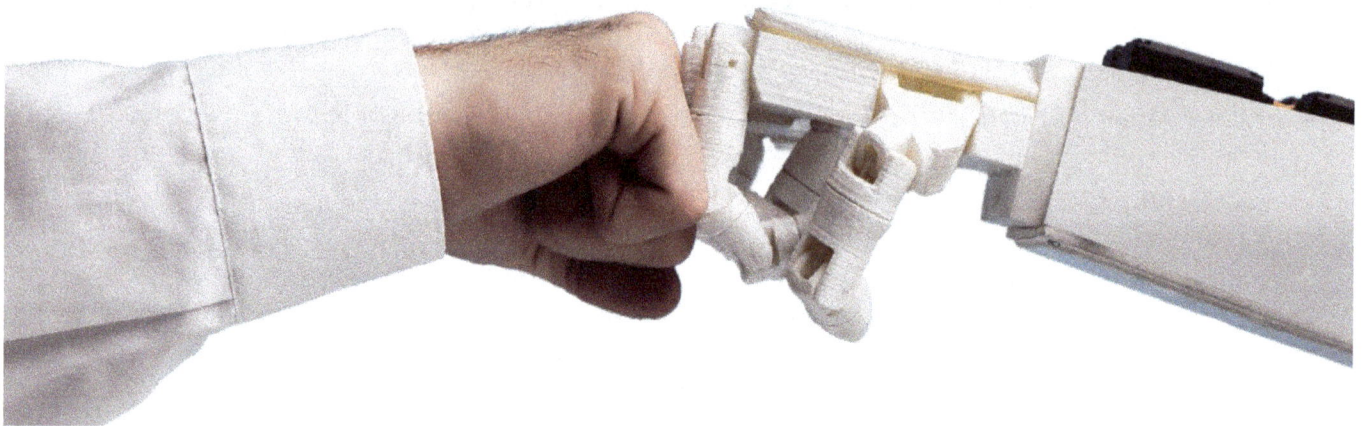

Calypso Ai

In a cozy breakout room of the recent Ai4 convention in Las Vegas, with an intimate gathering of 50 to 100 attendees, James White from CalypsoAi positioned himself center stage. Under the room's regular lighting, he paused for a brief second, drew a deep breath, then launched into his talk. With each word, his unwavering commitment to discussing the vast prospects and inherent hurdles of generative AI in today's enterprise realm was evident.

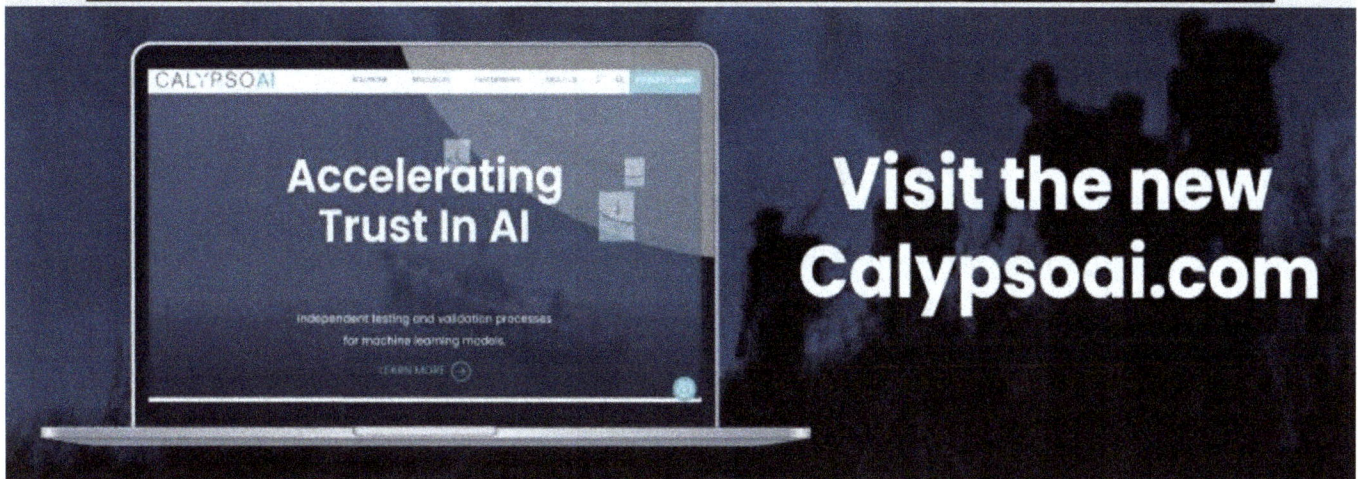

Generative AI is redefining boundaries," James began. "In economic terms alone, we're looking at a predicted $4.4 trillion in value generation annually. It's the pulse in boardrooms worldwide." He glanced at a report on the table: 1 in 5 executives are already integrating AI into their operations, and a whopping 70% are knee-deep in research about harnessing its capabilities.

However, James, with his astute technical acumen, was quick to pivot to the pressing challenges. "While AI's promise is vast, the risks associated with uncontrolled adoption are very real," he emphasized.

James talked about proprietary data breaches. Imagine algorithms inadvertently 'leaking' sensitive data, from intellectual properties to customer information. He touched upon the labyrinth of existing regulations, from GDPR in Europe to HIPAA in the U.S., underscoring the paramount importance of compliance. customer information. He touched upon the labyrinth of existing regulations, from GDPR in Europe to HIPAA in the U.S. underscoring the paramount importance of

compliance. "Transparency, traceability, and accountability are non-negotiable in the AI sphere," James highlighted. CalypsoAi isn't just offering a software solution; it's ensuring a comprehensive, fail-safe approach. Their robust framework ensures that the behavior of AI models remains consistent, traceable, and in compliance with both internal organizational standards and external regulatory bodies.

Furthermore, CalypsoAi's tech-driven monitoring system actively ensures that AI is used judiciously. From benign applications, like generating digital avatars, to more critical tasks like predictive analytics, the objective is to maintain integrity and purpose. James concluded, "In the AI domain, malicious threats are often sophisticated and camouflaged. Yet, with CalypsoAi's vigilant, tech-forward protective shield, businesses can confidently harness the potential of AI." The takeaway? As enterprises ride the wave of AI's transformative potential, with CalypsoAi's oversight, they can ensure that their voyage is not just impactful but also secure.

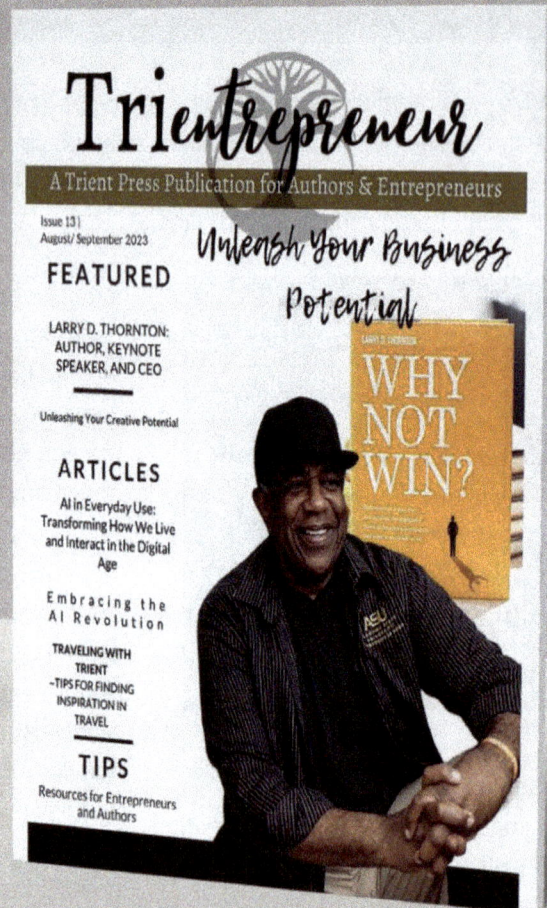

Shades of Success:

Shades of Success: Unpacking AI's Role in Fenty Beauty's Inclusivity Revolution

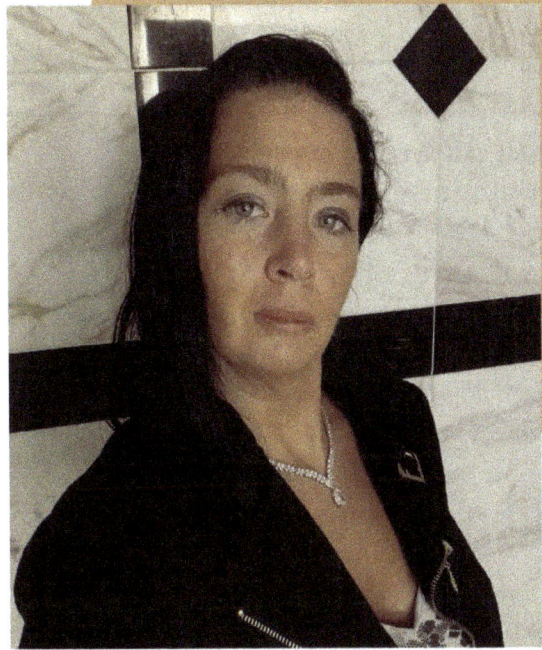

In the contemporary beauty industry, the quest for inclusivity has been a driving force, challenging conventions and pushing boundaries. Among these endeavors, the collaboration between AI and beauty stands out. This narrative seeks to explore how Fenty Beauty, a beacon of inclusivity, has harnessed AI to revolutionize the cosmetic world and potentially redefine several industries.

A Historical Oversight Corrected by AI

For years, the beauty industry, unintentionally or otherwise, marginalized specific skin tones by offering a limited palette of shades. This exclusion reflected a wider systemic issue: the deficiency of comprehensive data sets that cater to all skin shades, a crucial factor in computer vision problems. Without this extensive imagery data, the underrepresentation perpetuated.

Emmanuel Acheampong, during his passionate discourse at the Ai4 convention, noted: "The issue isn't with the algorithms, but with the data." He highlighted how products, specifically AI-based models, are only as effective as the data they are trained on. This sentiment was echoed throughout the meeting, emphasizing that without inclusive data, there remains an implicit bias in technology.

Melisa Ruscsak
Editor-in-Chief

Trient Press Magazine

SEPTEMBER/OCTOBER 2023

Integrating Data with Vision: Fenty Beauty's AI Journey

Fenty Beauty's initiative was commendable. Collaborating with AI pioneers, the company formulated a comprehensive data set that captured a myriad of skin shades. The intent was twofold: not only to enhance their product range but to ensure computer vision algorithms universally possess this diverse shade range. This endeavor allows smaller brands to refine their products and has the potential to introduce such inclusive technology to myriad industries.

A striking example is New Barn, a startup that crafts shapewear. By leveraging the AI models developed through Fenty Beauty's data, New Barn was able to reduce return rates by a staggering 70%. This demonstrated that AI's capabilities, when paired with extensive data, can dramatically optimize products and enhance user satisfaction.

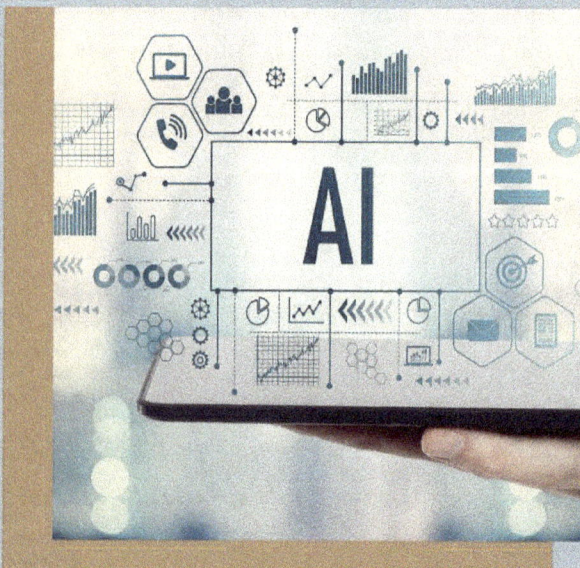

> "Fenty Beauty's collaboration with AI represents a transformative approach to inclusivity in the beauty industry, leveraging comprehensive datasets to challenge historical biases and inspire broader technological applications beyond cosmetics."

Expanding Horizons: Beyond Beauty

The implications of this technology are vast, transcending the beauty industry. One attendee, with a background in animation, expressed excitement about the technology's application in creating a diverse array of animated characters, showcasing AI's versatility. This perspective validates James White's assertion: "Our vision is that even though we started passionately in beauty, we could leverage the technology elsewhere because our data is universal."

Conclusion: A New Dawn in Inclusivity

In summation, the alliance between Fenty Beauty and AI is emblematic of a larger movement: using technological advancements to foster inclusivity and challenge historical biases. By leveraging AI and a robust dataset, Fenty Beauty has not only expanded its own product range but has also sown the seeds for an industry-wide revolution. As we continue to embrace the vast possibilities of AI, it is imperative that inclusivity remains at the forefront. As the conversation at the Ai4 convention showcased, the union of AI and data isn't just about enhancing products; it's about ensuring that technology, in all its facets, represents and serves everyone.

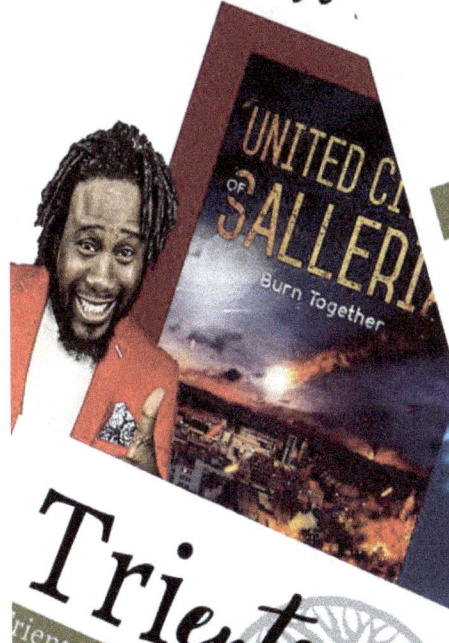

Tr entrepreneur

Tient Press Publication for Authors & Entrep

spring into o

Trientrepreneur

rient Press Publication for Authors & Entrepreneurs

December 2022

URED

RDNER
ootlight:
usiness

ce-
t it.)

Trientrepreneur

A Trient Press Publication for Authors & Entrepreneurs

Unleash Your Business Potential

Issue 13 |
August/ September 2023

FEATURED

LARRY D. THORNTON:
AUTHOR, KEYNOTE
SPEAKER, AND CEO

Unleashing Your Creative Potential

ARTICLES

AI in Everyday Use:
Transforming How We Live
nd Interact in the Digital
Age

r a c i n g   t h e
R e v o l u t i o n

**TRAVELING WITH
TRIENT**
–TIPS FOR FINDING
INSPIRATION IN
TRAVEL

TIPS

Resources for Entrepreneurs
and Authors

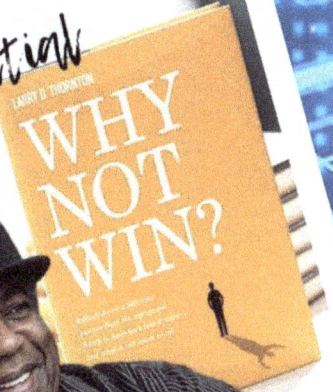

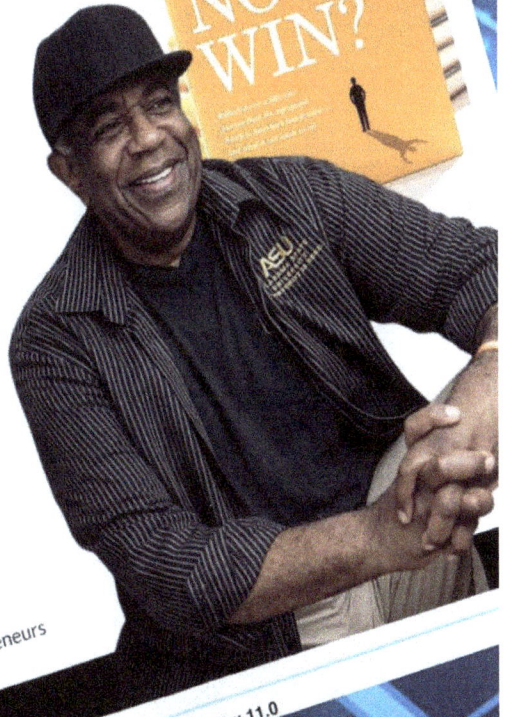

WHY
NOT
WIN?

8.250 x 11.0

Trientrepreneur

What's in your
Tool Box?

Silicon Stars:
Hollywood's Tryst with Artificial Intelligence

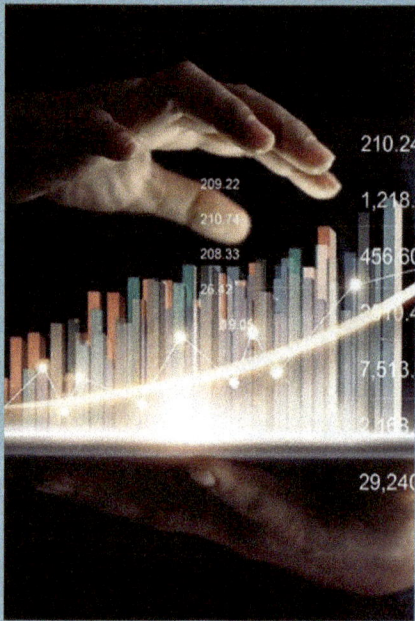

At the bustling Ai4 convention held in the dazzling city of Las Vegas, the convergence of innovation and imagination was palpable. Amidst a milieu of cutting-edge technological advancements, Hollywood, the bastion of dreams and storytelling, stood at an intriguing crossroad. Here, Robin Graham and Chris Ledoux, two luminaries in the film and television industry, presented a riveting discourse on the transformative impact of Artificial Intelligence on the world of filmmaking.

AI in the Film and TV Industry

Graham and Ledoux's opening remarks painted a vivid portrait of their long-standing association with the entertainment domain. With a combined experience spanning numerous projects over the years, their insights held a weight borne out of direct industry involvement.

Robin Graham, introducing himself alongside his business partner Chris Ledoux, spoke of their venture, "It offer than AI?" This enterprise specializes in providing hosting solutions tailored for AI training. While the duo briefly touched upon the technical prowess of their offering, such as disaggregated memory storage and GPU functionality, their keynote's true gravitas lay in the convergence of AI and film.

The duo emphasized the palpable tremors felt within the industry due to AI's influence. Recent news headlines highlighted the ripple effects caused by AI in Hollywood, including concerns over job security and the utilization of actors' likenesses. One particularly contentious point revolved around an alleged proposal by the American Film Committee. This proposal suggested that for a nominal fee, an actor's full 3D likeness could be digitally scanned and used indefinitely. Such an undertaking not only encroaches upon an actor's rights over their image but also poses an existential threat to the very foundation of acting as a profession. The ripple effect of AI doesn't stop there. With AI's capability to draft scripts within mere minutes, writers' roles are also potentially at risk.

How to achieve Tech Success #go2TGO

These rising concerns are not just limited to individual professionals. The broader infrastructure of the entertainment industry, including unions, finds itself grappling with the profound implications of AI. A reduction in workforce due to AI-driven processes potentially weakens union bargaining power, unsettling the existing dynamics.

The Evolving Landscape of AI in the Film and TV Industry

Historically, the silver screen has been the confluence of human creativity, expressions, and emotions. Yet, in recent times, there's an escalating integration of AI-driven processes that has stirred both trepidation and excitement. As Graham and Ledoux pointed out, Hollywood is grappling with the potential repercussions of AI on job security, the commoditization of actors' likenesses, and the destabilization of union powers. With AI now capable of scripting narratives within minutes and possibly replacing the need for human writers, the apprehension is palpable. Furthermore, the emerging practice of scanning actors to recreate their likenesses for perpetuity, all for a meager one-time payment, is unsettling for many.

However, beyond the foreboding shadows of AI lies a brighter perspective. The duo clarified that their discourse wouldn't dwell on the potential replacement of writers or actors but would spotlight how AI can be an invaluable ally in pre and post-production stages.

The Pioneering Tool: Streamlining Film Production

Chris Ledoux introduced an avant-garde tool designed to harness the prowess of language models for the benefit of the film industry. At its core, this tool isn't about usurping creative roles; it's about enhancing the organization, efficiency, and scalability of film production.

How does it work? Once a script is fed into their language model, the tool envisions and pre-visualizes the entire film. This is not just about storyboards or rough sketches but a comprehensive preview complete with voiceovers and scores. This digital incarnation allows directors to view, review, and refine their vision multiple times before a single scene is shot. Such a method can dramatically reduce inefficiencies and costs. The oft-quoted industry phrase "We'll fix it in post" reflects a glaring lack of pre-planning, leading to

hefty post-production expenses. Ledoux's solution squarely addresses this by laying the groundwork in the pre-production phase. One of the most revolutionary aspects of this tool lies in its logistical acumen. Once the pre-visualization is finalized, it offers a detailed blueprint to the crew, enumerating every prop, actor, and setup required for each scene. This meticulous planning can drastically reduce the quantum of overshot content, leading to substantial cost savings. Moreover, with the database integration, producers can factor in variables like tax credits, exchange rates, and local production costs to optimize the film's budget.

Reflections and Implications

The application of AI in Hollywood, as illustrated by Graham and Ledoux, is not a doomsday prophecy of machines replacing humans. Rather, it's a testament to the synergies that can be achieved when technology complements human creativity. By facilitating a more streamlined, cost-effective, and efficient filmmaking process, AI can amplify the realization of directors' visions, resulting in richer cinematic experiences.

It's also prudent to note that the current upheavals and strikes in the industry may not solely be about AI's infiltration but might also be reflective of deeper systemic financial issues. By leveraging AI tools like the one introduced by Ledoux, the industry can potentially steer towards more sustainable practices.

Concluding Thoughts

In the shimmering halls of the Ai4 convention in Las Vegas, the enthralling keynote by Graham and Ledoux captured the essence of a changing Hollywood. While Artificial Intelligence undeniably brings with it a host of concerns and challenges, it also holds the promise of a reimagined and efficient filmmaking process. As Hollywood continues its dance with technology, the narrative of its future is still being written, and it promises to be as compelling as the stories the industry has told for decades.

New Release

By: M.L. Ruscsak

Exploring the Ancient Pathways
of the Subconscious

Dreams of Babylon

M.L. Ruscsak

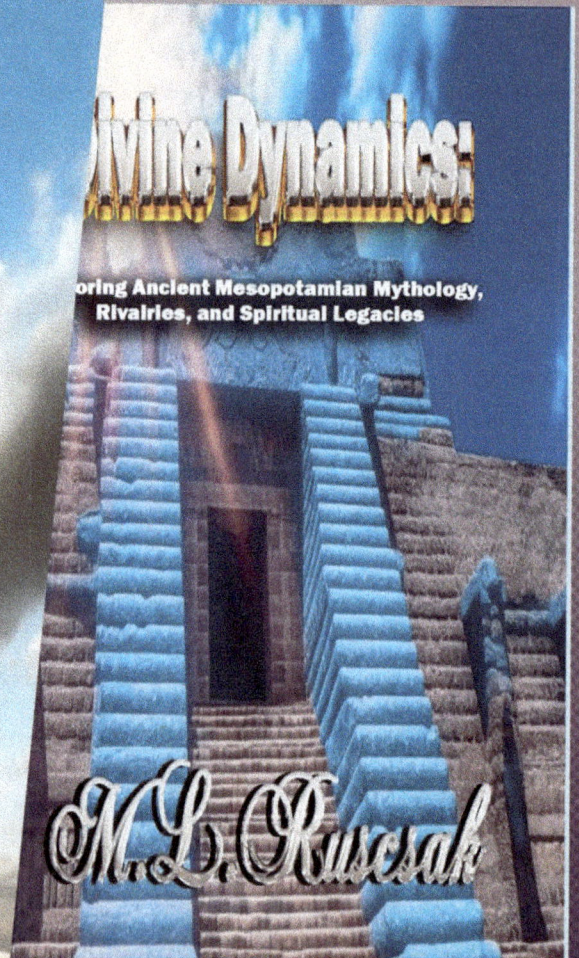

Divine Dynamics:

...oring Ancient Mesopotamian Mythology,
Rivalries, and Spiritual Legacies

M.L. Ruscsak

Trient Press®

AI4: UNITING THE GLOBAL AI ECOSYSTEM

Ai4 Las Vegas, 2023

When AI Became Our Next-Door Neighbor

Picture this: you're at your favorite coffee shop. You grab a seat next to a dude deeply engrossed in his laptop. You both strike up a conversation, and he begins telling you about this fantastic event he attended, Ai4. But instead of zoning out, you're hooked. Why? Because this isn't a sci-fi movie plot – it's the real deal. Let's unpack this.

IA Glimpse into Tomorrow's Tech-Centric World

Ai4 isn't just a futuristic buzzword or the latest tech fad. Dive deeper, and you'll find it's the epicenter of a technological renaissance. Picture it as a massive global summit, not with Aunt Betty sharing her pie recipes or Uncle Joe's fishing tales, but with the brightest minds unveiling the potential of Artificial Intelligence.

Remember when we marveled at the idea of the Internet? Or when touchscreens sounded like sci-fi? Now, both are as ordinary as your morning coffee. Similarly, Ai4 serves as a portal to tomorrow's wonders, bringing glimpses of technologies that will soon blend seamlessly into our daily lives.

Let's get techie for a moment. At Ai4, you'd witness AI-driven solutions like Deep Learning, which enables machines to process data at a depth humans can't. Or Neural Networks, which mimic our brain's architecture to solve complex problems. These aren't mere theories; they're technologies gearing up to redefine industries, from healthcare to finance, entertainment to transportation.

It's not just for the tech-savvy or Silicon Valley elites. Whether you're an entrepreneur seeking the next big innovation, a student with a curious mind, or someone who recently marveled at how their smart fridge suggested a recipe based on its contents (yes, that's AI!), Ai4 is the hub.

In essence, Ai4 isn't just about understanding machines. It's about reimagining a world where machines understand us. A world where technology is no longer a tool but a partner, amplifying our potential and simplifying the complex labyrinth of modern life. The future isn't just arriving; at Ai4, it's already here. So, let's delve in, explore, and co-create the AI-driven epoch that awaits us.

AI for All: Beyond Fiction to Functionality

At Ai4, we aren't merely delving into the realm of science fiction with sentient robots or dystopian futures. Instead, we're venturing into a tangible era of technologically-driven solutions. Visualize a world where gridlocked highways and bumper-to-bumper traffic become tales of the past. How, you ask? With vehicles leveraging Machine Learning algorithms to predict and adapt to traffic patterns, ensuring optimal routes are taken in real-time.

Consider this: doctors, instead of solely relying on symptoms and diagnostic tests, utilize Predictive Analytics.

By analyzing vast amounts of patient data, AI can forecast potential health anomalies, allowing medical professionals to intervene even before the onset of the first symptom.

The backbone of these advancements is an array of technological frameworks and processes. Deep Neural Networks, which mimic the structure of the human brain, process complex data to make intelligent decisions. Reinforcement Learning enables machines to learn from the environment and optimize actions based on feedback, much like teaching a dog new tricks. And Natural Language Processing ensures our digital assistants comprehend and respond to our everyday language, facilitating smoother human-machine interactions.

In essence, Ai4 is championing a future where AI doesn't just remain confined within the walls of research labs. It seamlessly integrates into our daily lives, transforming challenges into opportunities and optimizing our routines. This isn't the work of a wand; it's the power of Artificial Intelligence, tailored for everyone, everywhere.

The Human Heartbeat Behind AI's Digital Pulse

Whenever we broach the subject of AI, it's easy to get tangled in visions of cold, impersonal machines. And yes, there are valid concerns: What will become of jobs? How will our personal data be used? And, looming large above all, the fear: Could AI someday overshadow human intelligence?

However, platforms like Ai4 offer a gentle, poignant reminder that each line of code in AI's vast neural networks is birthed from human hands, human stories, and, most importantly, human intentions. AI isn't merely an outcome of rigorous mathematics and complex algorithms; it's a tapestry woven with human emotions, aspirations, and the profound desire to uplift our collective experience.

Take, for instance, my conversation with Sarah, a talented developer with a twinkle in her eye. As we sipped on lukewarm coffee, she narrated her journey into the realm of AI. It wasn't about creating the next big tech disruption or garnering applause in tech conferences. It was heartfelt and deeply personal. Sarah designed her first AI tool out of sheer love for her grandmother, aiming to simplify her weekly grocery shopping expeditions. There wasn't a hint of a grand scheme for world domination in her tale, just the genuine wish to make a beloved elder's life a smidgen more comfortable.

So, while AI's capabilities seem boundless and its potential colossal, it's essential to remember that its core beats with a human heart. Its progression is mapped out not by faceless entities but by individuals like Sarah, whose motivations are rooted in compassion, innovation, and the age-old human quest to better our world. In that, there's a comfort, a warmth, that only the human touch can bring to the digital realm.

AI isn't the Wild West.

Drawing the Lines: Navigating the AI Frontier

Contrary to the often frenzied media portrayal, the realm of AI is not akin to the lawless landscapes of the Wild West. Instead, imagine it as a rapidly growing frontier town, teeming with potential, but also in dire need of structure and boundaries. Attending events like Ai4 offers a deep dive into the heart of these pivotal conversations, emphasizing the imperative nature of regulations and guidelines in the vast world of artificial intelligence.

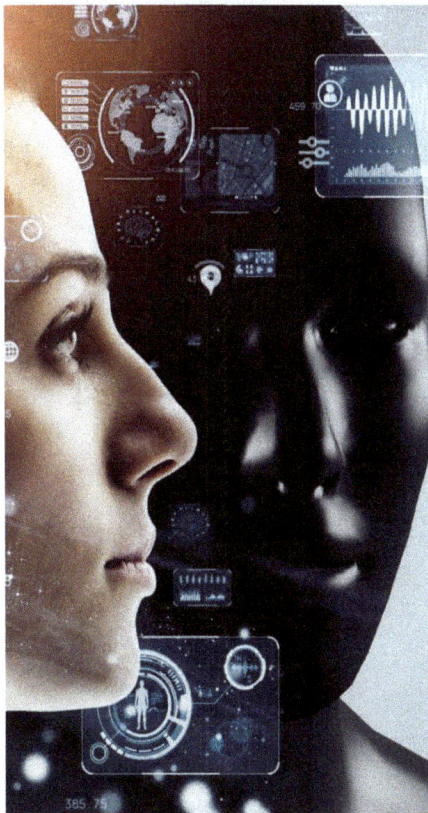

Setting these boundaries isn't about stifling innovation. Instead, it's about channeling AI's transformative power in ways that harmoniously align with human values and societal needs. Think of this process much like training a new pet. We bring pets into our homes, hoping they'll add joy, companionship, and even a sense of purpose. But without proper training, that same pet could potentially wreak havoc, from torn-up furniture to more serious transgressions. Similarly, AI, in its raw, unguided state, possesses the power to reshape facets of our daily lives, economies, and even sociopolitical landscapes in unpredictable ways.

Hence, the analogy of training holds weight. We aim to mold AI to serve us, to enhance our capabilities, and to coexist seamlessly in our ever-evolving world. The goal is not to dampen its potential but to ensure it remains a tool in our arsenal, a trusted ally, rather than an uncontrollable force with its own, potentially misaligned, objectives.

To that end, platforms like Ai4 are invaluable. They act as melting pots, where experts, ethicists, policymakers, and laypersons converge. Here, in the crucible of collaborative discussion, the future of AI is molded, ensuring it remains firmly tethered to our collective best interests, aspirations, and well-being.

All Aboard the AI Express

Picture this: a massive train called AI, fueled by the dreams, innovations, and aspirations of humanity. Contrary to popular belief, this isn't a locomotive steered by cold, emotionless machines. Instead, at its helm are passionate people, each with their unique stories, goals, and visions. We stand on the cusp of an era where every aspect of our lives, from mundane tasks to complex decision-making processes, is being influenced by AI. While the intricacies of its workings might seem daunting to most, its implications concern us all. Hence, whether you're a coding genius or someone who just learned how to use Siri, this train ride is yours too.

We're all passengers aboard this exhilarating journey into the future, each with a stake in where it's headed. When you come across discussions like those at Ai4 or other AI-centric platforms, don't just be a bystander. Engage, inquire, and immerse yourself. Our collective destiny is interwoven with the tapestry of AI's evolution.

> ### Suzy Welch once remarked, "Change is scary, but not changing is even scarier."

After all, the future isn't just something that awaits us. It's something we actively create. And with AI in the mix, that future is unfolding, moment by moment, right before our eyes.

Embark on a journey of wisdom and camaraderie at Dove and Dragon Radio. Tune in for riveting conversations spanning business strategies, travel tales, and more.

THE WORLD EVOLVES, RADIO TRANSFORMS.

WELCOME TO A NEW ERA OF AUDITORY EXPLORATION.

Trient Press.

DOVE AND DRAGON RADIO

Navigating Changes in Your Industry: Redefining the Spotlight: AI's Transformative Role in the Entertainment Renaissance

Welcome to the extraordinary world of Ai4, the preeminent AI for business community that unites the global AI ecosystem through a dynamic blend of events, media, and resources. Our mission is to provide a common framework for industries as we step into an era of responsible human-machine collaboration. Through our premium conferences, we offer multi-day experiences brimming with innovation, top-notch speakers, and AI companies at the forefront of transformation. Don't miss our upcoming event at MGM Grand Las Vegas, Nevada, from Aug 7-10. Join our esteemed Leadership Council, where influential members help shape our events and ensure we deliver cutting-edge information essential for AI leaders' success.

Much like in crypto trading, setting a risk threshold is vital for businesses navigating the AI space. Determining the right amount of risk a company can accommodate and pattern their strategies accordingly lays the groundwork for responsible AI implementation. Building a secure trading ecosystem for your AI integration, just as you would for your crypto investments, is equally crucial. Ensuring privacy, security, and control over your AI systems protects your assets from potential vulnerabilities.

Researching and understanding the specific risks associated with different AI technologies, much like exploring the nuances of various crypto coins, helps businesses make informed decisions. Diversifying your investment portfolio in AI solutions ensures that you don't place all your hopes on one technology, mitigating potential risks and maximizing opportunities.

Finally, having an exit strategy for AI integration is just as prudent as planning for an exit strategy in crypto trading. Recognizing the circumstances that may require a shift in allegiance to a different AI solution or even stepping back from certain technologies ensures companies can adapt and thrive in a rapidly changing environment.

AS WE DIVE INTO THE EVER-EVOLVING LANDSCAPE OF AI, IT'S CRUCIAL TO ACKNOWLEDGE THE RISKS AND OPPORTUNITIES THAT COME WITH IT. JUST AS IN THE CRYPTO TRADING WORLD, WHERE RISK MANAGEMENT IS ESSENTIAL, BUSINESSES TOO MUST ADOPT A LEVELHEADED APPROACH WHEN EMBRACING AI TECHNOLOGY. FROM THE EARLY STRUGGLES OF APPLE INC. TO ITS REMARKABLE SUCCESS TODAY, WE SEE THE POWER OF INNOVATION AND DETERMINATION IN TRANSFORMING FAILURES INTO TRIUMPHS.

As we continue our AI journey, let's embrace the lessons from the crypto trading world and incorporate risk management into our AI strategies. The way we respond to challenges and opportunities will be pivotal in shaping our success in the AI-powered future. With Ai4 as your trusted partner, we're here to guide you through this transformational journey, harnessing the full potential of AI and building a future that seamlessly blends human ingenuity with the limitless possibilities of technology. Together, we'll unlock a brave new world of innovation, collaboration, and progress. Welcome aboard!

Ai4 2023

Beyond Algorithms:
The Human Connection at AI Conferences

M.L. Ruscsak

Ever been to a family BBQ? That's what it feels like. Instead of discussing Aunt Sue's famous potato salad, you're diving into the ethics of machine learning or the potential of neural networks. And just like at the BBQ, it's not always about the main topic. Sometimes it's about sharing stories, laughing, and forming connections that go beyond the digital realm.

Imagine, for a second, standing in a room filled with people from every corner of the globe. Some are mathematicians, others are artists, and some might have just dipped their toes into the AI waters. But they're all there, united by one thing: the magic of Artificial Intelligence.

It's the human stories that stick with you. Like the young coder from Brazil who developed an AI model to help his village predict rainfall. Or the woman from Tokyo who's using AI to create music that speaks to the soul.

You know, it's funny. When most people think of AI, they imagine lines of code, complex algorithms, or maybe even robots. They're not wrong, but there's a piece of the puzzle that often goes overlooked: the humans behind the tech.

AI conferences aren't just a gathering of nerds. Trust me, I've been to a few. They're more like huge reunions. Reunions of brilliant minds from all walks of life, coming together with a shared passion.

However, let's step back for a moment. It's easy to get caught up in the allure of groundbreaking tech, but at the heart of it all lies something far more profound: our collective dreams, ambitions, and the shared vision of a future. This isn't merely about constructing smarter machines; it's about crafting a brighter, more inclusive tomorrow. The spark that lights up during these conferences goes beyond the confines of auditoriums and seminar rooms. Like a stone creating ripples in a pond, the impact of these discussions cascades, influencing sectors, societies, and the personal trajectories of countless individuals.

So, when headlines buzz with the latest AI marvel, take a moment. Pause and think about the human element that fueled it. Consider the camaraderie that blossomed over casual coffee chats, the intense debates that stretched into the wee hours, and the unified vision of melding technology's prowess with humanity's essence.

Suzy Welch's words, "Find your arena," resonate deeply with so many. It's that notion of finding a space where you genuinely belong, a place that ignites your passion and channels your strengths. For an ever-growing tribe of tech enthusiasts, innovators, and visionaries, AI conferences serve as that very arena. It's where boundaries aren't just acknowledged but challenged, where fresh ideas aren't just pondered but are birthed into existence, and where the line between the possible and impossible is frequently blurred.

If life ever leads you to the doorstep of an AI conference, seize the opportunity. Dive in headfirst. Because beyond the tech jargon and flashy demos, you'll discover something invaluable: a testament to human creativity, collaboration, and the bonds that tie us all together.

Malcolm Gladwell, with his knack for breaking down intricate phenomena, often talks about "tipping points." These are crucial junctures in time where seemingly small triggers catalyze significant shifts in the broader scheme of things. And in the grand timeline of technological evolution, AI conferences stand as prominent markers. They're not merely events; they're transformative moments propelling us toward a future we've long imagined.

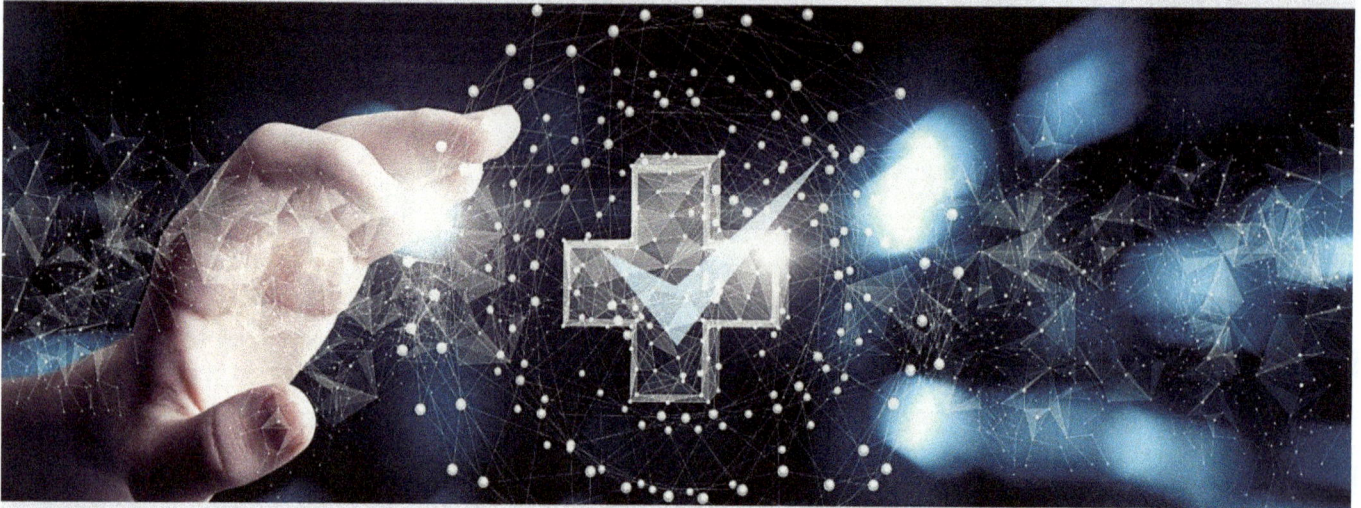

Coding Wellness:

The Rise of AI in Healthcare

You ever chat with a friend about something super sci-fi, like a robot doctor? Well, we're not exactly there... but we're closer than you might think. Imagine: A world where your next check-up might just involve some pretty clever tech.

You know that moment Malcolm Gladwell talks about – the tipping point? That split second when the ordinary becomes extraordinary. That's what's happening in healthcare right now, all thanks to AI.

Now, I get it. Hearing "AI" and "healthcare" in the same sentence can sound a tad... cold. Machines, algorithms, data – doesn't quite give you the warm and fuzzies, does it? But here's the thing Suzy Welch would probably say: "Find the human side of the story." And trust me, it's there.

Picture this: A young woman named Lisa, living miles away from any hospital. She's got a lingering cough, and in the pre-AI days, she'd probably just hope for the best. Now? A simple app on her phone listens to her cough, and bam! It tells her she needs to see a doc. No, it's not a magic 8-ball; it's AI making healthcare accessible.

And those terrifying waits for test results? AI's cutting those down big time. No more anxiety-filled nights, hoping everything's alright. The tech's scanning, analyzing, and spotting stuff even before the doc's morning coffee.

But here's where it really hits home. Remember Aunt Jenny, who fought that tough battle with cancer? Imagine if her doctors had AI to spot those tiny, almost invisible signs early on. Those are the real stories. The real magic. It's not just about faster and better. It's about more moments with the people we love.

I had a chat with Dr. Ramirez, who's right at the heart of this AI healthcare revolution. Over a steamy cup of joe, he told me, "It's like I've got this superpower now. I can see more, know more, and most importantly, do more for my patients."

But (and there's always a but, right?) with great power, comes great responsibility. The big question? Ethics. How do we ensure that this super tech benefits everyone and doesn't just become another luxury for the few?

It's an exciting time, my friends. AI in healthcare isn't some distant dream. It's here. It's now. It's real. And the beautiful part? Behind all that code, all those algorithms, there's a heartbeat. A human touch. A desire to make tomorrow just a tad bit better than today.

So, the next time you're at the doc's and they mention some newfangled AI tool, lean in. Listen. Because that's not just tech talk. It's the sound of the future. And trust me, it sounds pretty darn good.

Romantic Thriller
By: TINA MAURINE

DARE
to THE
BREATHE

TINA MAURINE

Trient Press

Traveling with Trient

TRIPPING THROUGH TRIENT:

FROM MGM'S GRANDEUR TO LUXOR'S LEGACY, NAVIGATING AI4 AND EMBARKING ON THE SACRED EGYPTIAN ODYSSEY

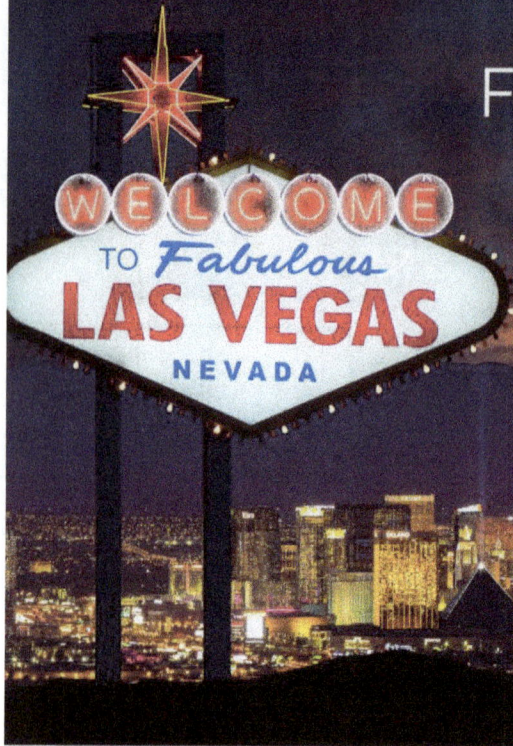

Imagine this: You're standing amidst the glittering lights of Las Vegas, surrounded by the grandeur of the iconic MGM Grand. Just a few steps away, the alluring silhouette of the Luxor pyramid beckons. This isn't just any other Sin City escapade—it's a fusion of future tech and ancient wonders, all interwoven seamlessly.

The MGM Grand, with its promise of luxury, sets the stage. It's where AI enthusiasts and industry giants gather annually for the AI4 conference—a melting pot of minds eager to shape the digital future. Here, amidst the opulence, discussions range from the mundane to the revolutionary, and the palpable excitement is impossible to ignore.

The Luxor, draped in its opulent Egyptian finery, stands as the ideal locale to unveil the first four modules of "The Sacred Journey" class—its essence resonating deeply within the King Tut exhibit. On the other hand, the MGM Grand paints a contrasting picture, embodying the quintessential Sin City vibe, with every corner revealing unabashed extravagance. Its eateries and shops promise a tantalizing experience, though the accommodations leave one yearning for more luxury. However, a shift occurs upon entering its convention center. Suddenly, the third floor is awash with the language of the future: Artificial Intelligence.

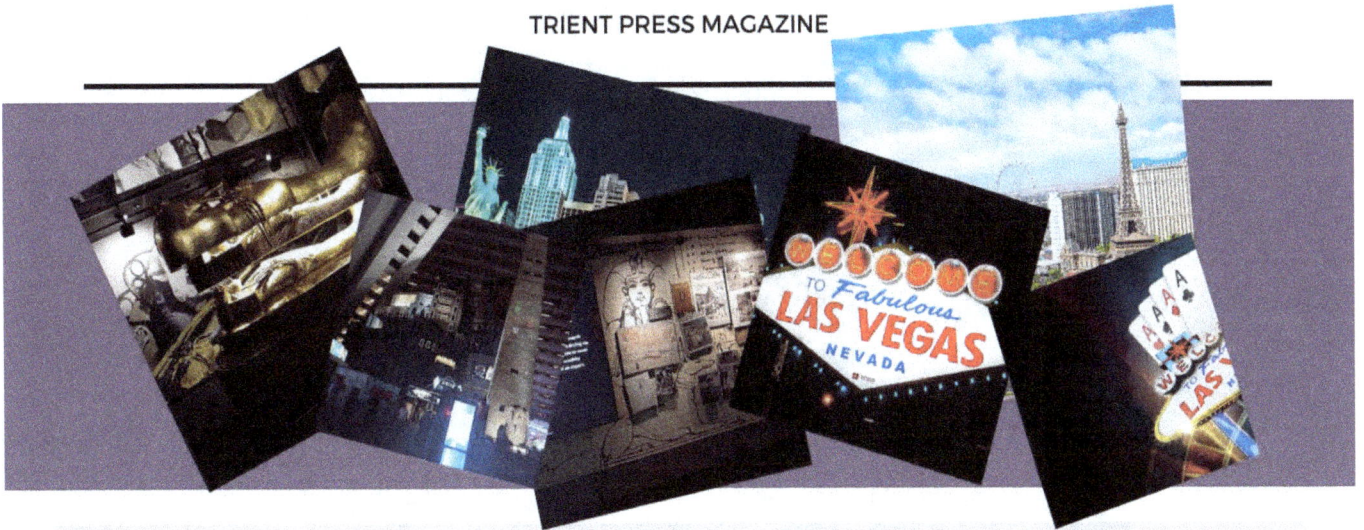

There, you'll hear passionate debates about the latest in AI. Whispers of "Have you attended that neural network session?" or exclamations like "Deep learning will revolutionize our industry!" echo throughout. These conversations underscore the event's mission: forging new frontiers in technology.

Yet, just a stone's throw away, the allure of ancient times beckons. The Luxor, with its magnificent pyramid, is where yesteryears intertwine with today. Not merely a visual treat, it symbolically connects the groundbreaking discussions of AI4 with the timeless allure of ancient Egypt.

It's within this setting that The Sacred Journey class unfolds, offering participants a gateway to the mysteries of ancient Egyptian culture. As AI strives to shape our future, this class serves as a bridge to a past replete with myths and miracles.

Under the blazing Nevada sky, the juxtaposition is evident. To one side lies the realm of coding and algorithms, shaping our tomorrow. On the other, stories of majestic pharaohs and the vast Nile, invoking memories of great civilizations.

Both establishments, MGM Grand and Luxor, signify an important truth: our aspirations for the future are deeply rooted in our past. While AI4 sketches a blueprint for the technological horizon, it does so under the vigilant gaze of ancient tales and hieroglyphs.

This dichotomy encapsulates the spirit of Las Vegas. A city of dreams, both new and revisited, where today's marvels are a testament to yesterday's tales.

So, amidst the shimmering neon and the gentle desert breeze, remember: stories are etched at every turn. From the tech marvels at AI4 to the haunting echoes of Pharaohs, Las Vegas offers an unparalleled odyssey. Embark, and let the city narrate tales of modern magnificence and bygone splendor.

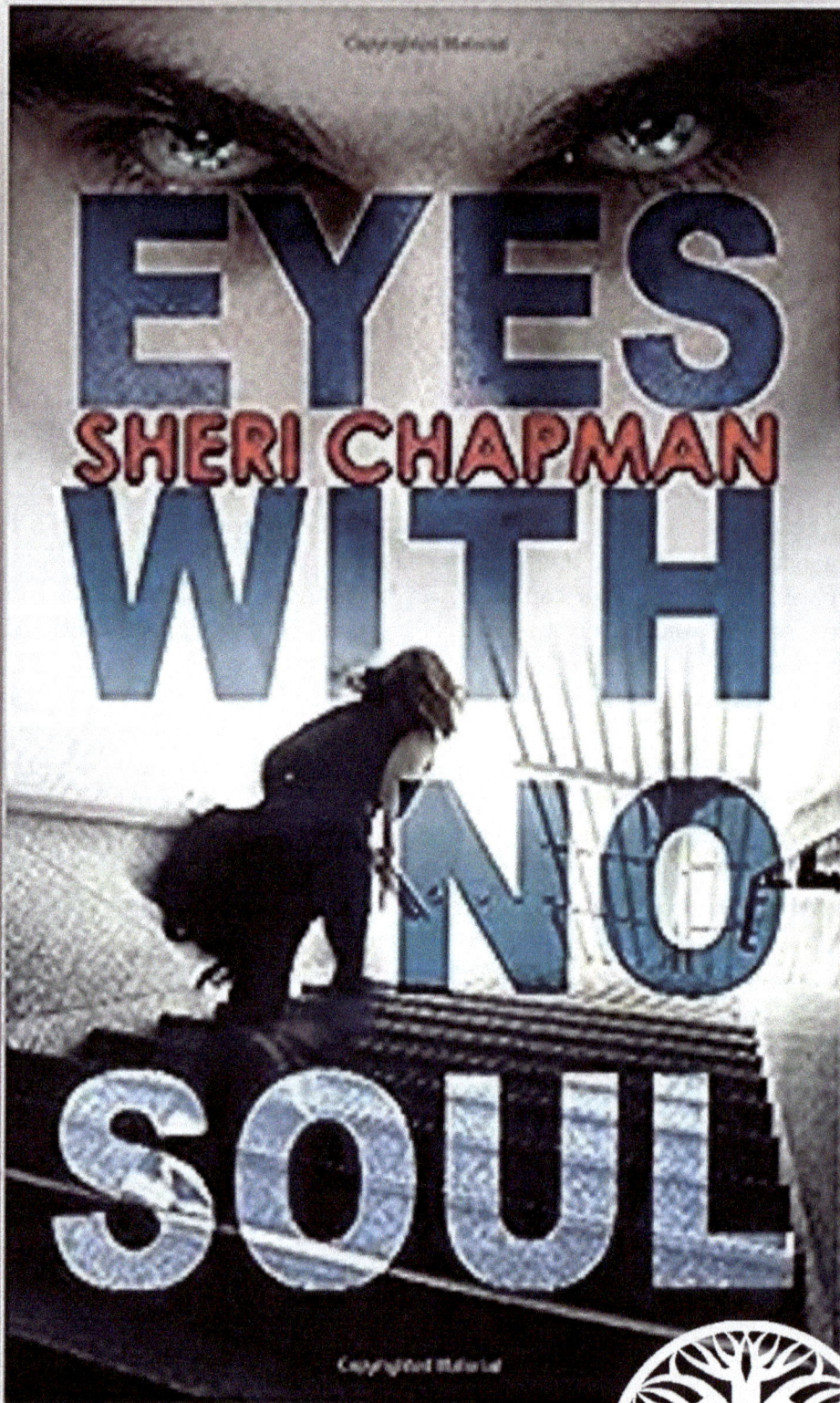

EYES
SHERI CHAPMAN
WITH NO SOUL

SHERI CHAPMAN

Trient Press

CULINARY CROSSROADS:
A DECADENT DETOUR AT
HELL'S KITCHEN

Review
Restaurant Review

By: M.L. Ruscsak

After an enriching exploration of the Luxor and its captivating King Tut exhibit, my feet led me to the doors of Hell's Kitchen. With expectations of winding down with a tranquil dinner, I stepped in, hoping for a culinary experience reflective of the restaurant's esteemed reputation.

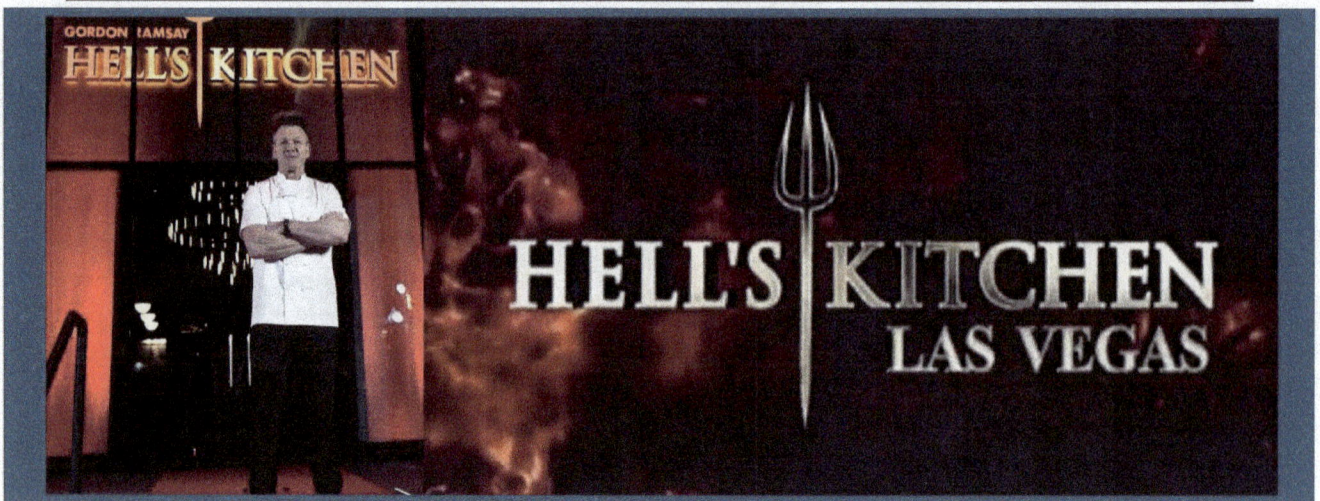

My selection for the evening, the Braised Short Rib paired with the tantalizing Hell's Red Infusion drink, was nothing short of spectacular. The melt-in-your-mouth rib, complemented by the yukon potato cake, bloomsdale spinach, crispy onion rings, and the rich beef jus, was a symphony of flavors and textures. On the other hand, the Hell's Red Infusion—a harmonious blend of apple, strawberry, rhubarb puree, simple syrup, and fever-tree ginger beer—was the perfect refreshing companion to the hearty main course.

Yet, as I took in the ambiance, I couldn't help but notice the walls adorned with past winners of the famed Hell's Kitchen reality TV show—a delightful touch for aficionados of the series.

However, my solo dining status meant I was ushered to the bar instead of the primary dining area. Understandable, given the establishment's position as one of Vegas's culinary crown jewels.

"*After immersing oneself in the historical grandeur of the Luxor, there's a culinary haven awaiting in Hell's Kitchen. Here, amidst the vibrant tapestry of flavors and the legacy of culinary champions, one realizes that the true essence of Las Vegas lies not just in its glittering facades, but in shared experiences that tantalize the senses and linger in the memory.*" - M.L. Ruscsak

The culinary centerpiece of my evening was the Braised Short Rib, a dish that boasted exquisite craftsmanship and flavor execution. Each bite of the rib was tender and succulent, effortlessly pulling apart under the gentlest nudge of the fork. The rib was perfectly paired with a yukon potato cake which, with its soft interior and slightly crisp exterior, created a delightful textural juxtaposition.

The bloomsdale spinach added a hint of earthiness, while the crispy onion rings introduced an additional layer of crunch, and the rich beef jus enveloped everything in a velvety embrace. This was indeed a plate where each element had been thoughtfully curated to elevate the dish to a gastronomic artwork.

The bar area, with its constant flurry of activity, presented an ambiance that was quite different from the calm and secluded dinner setting I had imagined. The clinking of glasses, bartenders concocting a multitude of colorful libations, and spirited chatter from patrons transformed my meal into a more dynamic experience. While I had anticipated a serene backdrop to my meal, the vibrancy of the bar had its own allure, adding an unexpected dimension to my evening.

However, the heart of Hell's Kitchen lies not just in its setting, but in its culinary artistry—and that remained undiminished. Each dish, meticulously crafted, was a testament to the restaurant's commitment to gastronomic brilliance. The minor detour in seating didn't detract from the essence of what Hell's Kitchen truly represents: a confluence of top-tier culinary innovation and the rich legacy of a television show that has, over the years, become synonymous with culinary drama and triumph.

"In the vibrant whirl of Hell's Kitchen's bar, amidst the symphony of clinks and chatter, lies a culinary masterpiece waiting to be discovered. As the legacy of a revered TV show melds with gastronomic finesse, one is reminded: the essence of dining is not just in the flavors, but in the shared memories crafted around the table."

For anyone contemplating a visit to this renowned eatery in the heart of Las Vegas, I'd offer a slice of personal insight: dining is an experience best shared. While the flavors and aromas are undoubtedly a feast for the senses, the joy of breaking bread is amplified when done in the company of friends or loved ones. So, as you make your reservation, consider rallying a group. Not only might it secure you a prime spot in the main dining arena, but it also provides the perfect setting to collectively immerse in, and celebrate, a culinary spectacle that Hell's Kitchen so masterfully delivers.

M&M WORLD LAS VEGAS: A COLORFUL OASIS IN THE DESERT

Amid the glitz and glamour of the Las Vegas Strip, there's a beacon of color and sweetness that beckons to both the young and the young-at-heart: M&M World. This isn't just a store; it's a four-story tribute to one of America's most beloved candies.

As you step into M&M World, you're immediately enveloped in a rainbow of colors. Walls lined with M&M's, available in every shade imaginable, offer a customization experience like no other. Want to fill a bag with only your favorite colors or mix and match to create your personal palette? The choice is yours!

But it's not just about the candy. The merchandise available ranges from quirky and fun apparel to collectible items, each showcasing the M&M characters we've all come to adore. Whether you're looking for a memorable keepsake or a unique gift, there's something for every M&M aficionado.

One of the highlights of the store is the 3D movie, "I Lost My M in Vegas." This short, family-friendly film offers a fun diversion and provides a lighthearted backstory to our colorful candy friends.

As you navigate through the different levels, you'll encounter interactive displays, a personalization station where you can imprint M&M's with your messages, and even a replica of Kyle Busch's #18 M&M's race car.

Located just next to the MGM Grand, M&M World Las Vegas provides a delightful break from the usual casino-hopping. It's a nostalgic trip down memory lane for adults and a wonder-filled adventure for children. So, if you find yourself amidst the neon lights and ringing slot machines, take a detour to this chocolate haven. Dive into a world of color, taste, and pure joy - all wrapped up in a candy-coated shell.

Vegas Golden Shrimp with Neon Risotto

INGREDIENTS

8 SERVINGS

FOR THE SHRIMP:
- 12 LARGE SHRIMP, PEELED AND DEVEINED
- 2 TBSP OLIVE OIL
- 1 GARLIC CLOVE, MINCED
- ZEST AND JUICE OF 1 LEMON
- PINCH OF EDIBLE GOLD DUST OR GOLD LEAF FOR GARNISH (OPTIONAL)
- SALT AND PEPPER TO TASTE

FOR THE NEON RISOTTO:
- 1 CUP ARBORIO RICE
- 4 CUPS CHICKEN OR VEGETABLE BROTH, KEPT WARM
- 1 SMALL ONION, FINELY CHOPPED
- 2 TBSP UNSALTED BUTTER
- 1/4 CUP WHITE WINE
- 1/2 CUP GRATED PARMESAN CHEESE
- NEON FOOD COLORING (BLUE, PINK, AND GREEN)
- SALT TO TASTE

DIRECTIONS

SHRIMP PREPARATION:

- IN A MIXING BOWL, COMBINE THE OLIVE OIL, MINCED GARLIC, LEMON ZEST, LEMON JUICE, SALT, AND PEPPER.
- ADD THE SHRIMP TO THE MARINADE AND LET THEM SIT FOR ABOUT 15 MINUTES.
- HEAT A SKILLET OVER MEDIUM-HIGH HEAT. ADD THE MARINATED SHRIMP AND COOK UNTIL THEY ARE PINK AND OPAQUE, ABOUT 2-3 MINUTES ON EACH SIDE. SET ASIDE.

PLATING:

- USING A ROUND MOLD (OR A COOKIE CUTTER), PLACE ONE COLOR OF THE RISOTTO AT A TIME, LAYERING THEM TO CREATE A TRICOLORED NEON EFFECT.
- ARRANGE THE SHRIMP AROUND THE RISOTTO.
- IF USING, GENTLY APPLY THE EDIBLE GOLD DUST OR GOLD LEAF TO THE SHRIMP TO GIVE THEM A LUXURIOUS SHEEN.
- SERVE IMMEDIATELY.

RISOTTO PREPARATION:

- IN A LARGE PAN OVER MEDIUM HEAT, MELT THE BUTTER AND SAUTÉ THE ONION UNTIL TRANSLUCENT.
- ADD THE ARBORIO RICE AND STIR CONTINUOUSLY UNTIL THE RICE IS WELL-COATED WITH THE BUTTER AND HAS A SLIGHT GOLDEN HUE.
- POUR IN THE WHITE WINE AND STIR UNTIL IT'S MOSTLY EVAPORATED.
- BEGIN ADDING THE WARM BROTH, ONE LADLE AT A TIME, STIRRING CONSTANTLY AND ALLOWING EACH ADDITION TO BE ABSORBED BEFORE ADDING THE NEXT.
- ONCE THE RICE IS AL DENTE AND HAS A CREAMY CONSISTENCY, STIR IN THE PARMESAN CHEESE.
- DIVIDE THE RISOTTO INTO THREE PARTS. ADD A DIFFERENT NEON FOOD COLORING TO EACH PORTION AND MIX WELL UNTIL YOU ACHIEVE THE DESIRED VIBRANT HUE FOR EACH.
- SEASON EACH PORTION WITH SALT AS NEEDED.

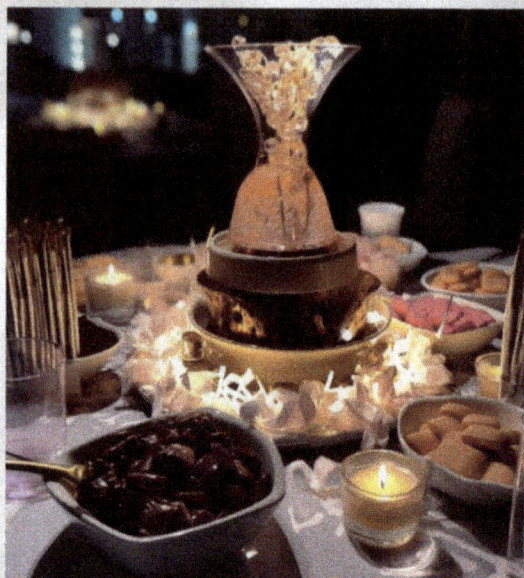

VEGAS GLITZ & GLAM CHOCOLATE FOUNTAIN FONDUE

Capturing the exuberance and splendor of Las Vegas, this dessert mimics the cascading lights of the city with a rich chocolate fountain and an array of colorful dippable delights.

Ingredients

For the Chocolate Fountain:

- 24 oz. high-quality dark chocolate
- 3/4 cup heavy cream
- 2 tbsp unsalted butter
- 1/4 cup orange liqueur (such as Grand Marnier or Cointreau)
- Edible gold flakes for garnish

Dippables:

-
- Strawberries, washed and dried
- Cubes of pound cake or angel food cake
- Large marshmallows
- Pretzel rods
- Sliced bananas
- Edible glitter in neon colors (like blue, pink, green, and yellow)

Directions

Preparing the Chocolate Fountain:
If you have a chocolate fountain machine, set it up according to the manufacturer's instructions.
In a heat-proof bowl over a pot of simmering water (double boiler), melt the chocolate, ensuring the water doesn't touch the bottom of the bowl.
Once the chocolate starts melting, add in the heavy cream, butter, and orange liqueur. Stir continuously until the mixture is smooth and well combined. Transfer the molten chocolate to the fountain and turn it on.

Dippables Preparation:
Arrange your dippables on a platter.
For an added touch of Vegas glitz, dust the strawberries, marshmallows, and banana slices with the edible glitter in various neon colors. Ensure the glitter adheres well. The contrast of the edible neon glitter against the dark cascading chocolate will mimic the neon lights against the night sky in Vegas.

Place the platter of dippables next to the chocolate fountain. As a final touch, sprinkle some edible gold flakes into the flowing chocolate to add that touch of opulence reminiscent of the lavish nature of Las Vegas. Guests can dip their chosen items into the fountain, letting the rich chocolate coat each piece before enjoying the sweet delight.

www.ingramcontent.com/pod-product-compliance
Lightning Source LLC
Chambersburg PA
CBHW051801200326
41597CB00025B/4640